Choose only Love

The Way of Being

BOOK VII

Messages from A Choir of Angels
Received by Sebastián Blaksley

TAKE HEART PUBLICATIONS

ELIGE SOLO EL AMOR | CHOOSE ONLY LOVE

Publication in English authorized by
Fundación amor vivo, a nonprofit organization, Argentina
Av. Libertador 16434
San Isidro
Buenos Aires, Argentina
www.fundacionamorvivo.org

TAKE HEART PUBLICATIONS
13315 Buttermilk Bend
North San Juan, CA 95960
www.takeheartpublications.com
ISBN 978-1-58469-691-9
Cover and editorial design by Alejandro Arrojo
Computer production by
Patty Arnold, *Menagerie Design and Publishing*
Manufactured in the United States of America

Choose only Love

The Way of Being

Table of contents

A Special Note about Gender

God has no gender. The masculine/feminine duality of personality is a human attribute. And yet, God is both masculine and feminine, for God is All. As All, God is both as personal as you and as impersonal as "It" or "Principle." Human beings can relate more intimately to a personal God than an impersonal one, and so in his lifetime Jesus created the idea of "God the Father," which casts God as a loving presence, and humans as part of a Divine Family. During Jesus' time, the culture could only accept a masculine figure; and ever since, much of the world has related to God as masculine in both imagery and in language. I grew up in a Catholic society in which God was universally referred to as "He." That tradition is reflected in the first three books of *Choose Only Love*.

In Book IV, however, God more fully revealed Herself: *"Until now, God Himself, in His infinite knowledge, wanted to show Himself in the world as Father, as well as the love that He is. But from now on She wants to show Herself as Mother, not only as wisdom. The 'feminine' of God will come to light more and more every day."* Thus the reader will notice that the language of the final four books in this series reflects both the masculine and feminine natures of God.

Choose Only Love leads us to grow in breadth of heart, to a greater degree of inclusion—including the idea of who or what God is. The reader can observe Father-Mother God merge into unity. Book VII culminates a journey in which we receive the unfathomable vastness of the being that we re-ally are—the

Christ. Then we embrace everything and everyone in the Divine Love that we truly are, inclusive in God's way.

~ Sebastián Blaksley, December 2021

A Message from Sebastián

These messages are for everyone and for all times, in spite of the limitation of human words, which can separate. Love includes everything we are. It takes us beyond our ideologies, cultures, educations, personalities, and beliefs, towards what cannot be expressed in words because love is beyond all limits. But to reach us effectively, the angels express their universal love using concrete symbols—in this case, words. We each come out of a particular cultural context. I am a lay person living in the 21st century, born in Argentina, with a Catholic education, and am very devoted to my faith. Therefore the flavor of these messages reflects my Catholic orientation; however, I clearly understood that love is universal and addressed to everyone and everything. Love is always inclusive.

As Jesus says in Book 5 of this series:

It is important that you remember that names, like words, have no meaning of their own in relation to the realm of divine truth. Do not forget that love has no words. However, in the plane of perceptions, names, like words, can mean a lot. Names that are used, such as Jesus, Mary, Holy Spirit, and God, have been endowed with many meanings over the centuries. We cannot escape the laws of perception while living in the world; nor is there any reason to do so. The love of God does not overlook anything in your world, but rather joins with it, and from that union, transforms it, together with you, so that the truth that is beyond every word shines freely.

I hope with all my heart that you feel included in the embrace of God's love through these messages from Heaven. But merely reading them will not bring you to Heaven's gate; rather, they are a port of departure or springboard from which you are encouraged daily to express with your particular voice the Divine Love that lives in you—increasingly to make known that part of love that only you can manifest.

If you are able to understand the words and symbols of this work as a means and not as an end, and receive these messages primarily with the heart rather than the thinking mind, you will go beyond the symbols towards the love that they evoke. You will begin to remember your first love, that is, for God. These writings are a love letter from God the Father/Mother to His/Her beloved daughters and sons. It is directed to the healing of memory so that, once healed, the remembered love that has no beginning or end shines in you.

I. How It Originated

On October 3, 2018, a presence that was all love and whose magnificence, beauty, and benevolence cannot be described, came to me suddenly in a way I had never before experienced. I understood with perfect clarity that it was the glorious Archangel Raphael. He introduced himself saying, "I am the medicine of God." He told me to pray a particular prayer for nine days. Through inner inspiration he also dictated certain intentions for me to pray. The prayers consisted of five Our Fathers, five Hail Marys, and five Glories, just as these prayers are presented in the Catholic Church, to which I belong.

On October 13, the day after finishing this novena of prayer, I began to receive glorious visits from a choir of countless angels of God accompanied by Archangel Raphael and Archangel Gabriel. Their love and beauty were indescribable. Through the choir came the Voice of Christ, expressed in an ineffable form and as images, shown in symbols visible to the spirit. I put the meaning of these images into written words, then into voice recordings.

Each visitation was the same: First I received the images and heard the music that the choir presents, then the chorus departed while Archangels Raphael and Gabriel remained as custodians, or loving presences, until the message or session in question was transcribed.

The glorious Archangel Raphael is the one who guides me in the transcription, assuring that the message is properly received and that what is shown can be passed from image to word. Archangel Gabriel is the loving custodian of everything that concerns the work, not only in reference to the manifestation itself and to the writings, but to everything that arises and will arise from them.

The messages, or sessions, are shown to me as a picture of great beauty in which each form (which has no form) is in itself a voice, a "sound-image." What I hear is like the rhythmical twanging of a harp that becomes translated into words. This tune is a vibration of celestial music whose frequency is unlike the sounds of the world. It is a kind of "vibration-frequency" that the soul knows perfectly well and that I recognize with certainty as the voice of the Lamb of God. Once everything is transcribed in written and spoken words, then the chorus arrives in all its glory once again, as if they were coming to seek the most holy Archangels Raphael and Gabriel. Then all together they retire, singing a hosanna to the Christ of God.

That hosanna sung by the choir of angels is a majestic song of praise and gratitude to the Creator for the infinite mystery of love that is the Second Coming. It is a prelude to His coming. If humankind were able to understand in all its magnitude the ineffable mystery of love that is the Second Coming of Christ, we would eternally sing the mercies of God in union with all the angels.

In cases where the Virgin Mary Herself or Jesus Christ are present in their human and divine person and communicate directly, the choir of angels is muted with love, in a silence that is sacred. Pure expectation, so to speak, surrounds their blessed presences. The angels bow their heads, cast their eyes downward, and are caught up in an ecstasy of love, veneration, and contemplation. Nothing and no one dares, nor could, interrupt the holy silence in which the universe is submerged before the sovereign presence of Mary and Jesus when they speak directly to our souls. This is because that space of dialogue between Christ and the soul is inviolable. It is the sacred temple of the intimacy of the soul with God.

When Archangel Raphael makes himself present to me and begins the process of translating images and symbols into written words, my will is fused into one will with him. We are one and the same will. There is no "you" and "me." And yet, even in that unity, there is the consciousness that I am I, and he is he: two persons with the same will, the same consciousness of being, in a single holy purpose. My thinking mind is silenced in this absorption of my being into the being of all true being, which we share as a unit. My consciousness and his become one. What the will of one says to be done, is done. There is no distance between the "be done" and its effect.

The rest of my humanity responds humbly. There is no resistance. There is only a flow of words coming from the Mind of Christ, as if it were from a spring that flows from the top of a mountain. This torrent of Grace made into words makes my fingers fly with speed and precision that far surpasses that of my ordinary writing. The soul remains ecstatic with love and with a single desire—to remain forever fused with the beloved Christ, being of our being and of all true being.

During the visitations my whole being is bathed in great peace and joy, like being embraced by universal love. But after concentrating on putting the message into words, the body shows great fatigue. It seems that it is difficult for it to sustain the energy I receive. The part of the manifestation that includes the chorus of angels, the voice, and the images is something that can happen at any time, place, or in any circumstance. However, the transcription of the symbols received into written words and then spoken and recorded can be delayed until I can make myself available to do so. It may be immediately afterwards or several days later.

The main message of this work could be summarized as follows: The time for a new humanity has arrived, a humanity that is ready to manifest the living Christ in each of us. We are, each of us, Christ. This is the truth about us, even if we perceive ourselves differently. We are already prepared to be able to live life in the certainty that says: I no longer live, but it is Christ who lives in me. Helping us to realize this truth in our lives, here and now, is what this manifestation is about. All of Heaven will help us in this holy purpose, since it is the Second Advent itself.

II. A Description of the Manifestations

When the Archangels come, they come without wings. They are like humans wearing tunics. Raphael's tunic is green, edged with gold. Gabriel's tunic is pink, almost white, edged with yellow. Both tunics are majestic, appearing as if made of a very precious silk.

Their faces are cheerful and radiant, with very light yellowish skin. Both have shoulder-length, golden blond hair and their eyes are green. They each have unique facial features. Their bodies are radiant with serene glowing light that generates peace and a great sense of beauty and harmony.

Many of the angels in the Chorus of Angels have light pink and light blue tunics. Others have light gold, but all are pastel colors, again with a serene luminosity. A few have green robes as if they were emeralds but a little lighter.

The permanent happiness that angels exhibit is remarkable. Everything is joy with them. One day they told me that they radiate perpetual happiness because they always share happiness.

The angels are always surrounded by white and majestic light, as if they live in an eternal mid-day of love and light. They are accompanied by music, as though a celestial choir is singing in all corners of the universe, like the sound of millions of harps playing in unison, forming a harmonious symphony of great beauty.

The angelic vibrations are of such a degree that they calm the mind and the heart, and give peace. One knows, without knowing how, that this vibration is simultaneously prayer and praise. Each part of the universe (creation) sings a song of gratitude for it having been called into existence, as though it has music inside that is a prayer to the Creator. The human soul had stopped hearing this celestial music but will begin to hear it again when it returns to the Father's house. Though forgotten, this song is forever loved by souls that love the Father and Creator.

The ineffable, inexpressible beauty of these visions of angels and archangels submerges the soul in an ecstasy of love and rapture in which one's whole being participates. No joy or happiness on Earth compares with the ecstasy that a vision of the greatness, magnanimity, and beauty of the angels and archangels generates.

Angelic intelligence is of such a degree that it surpasses all worldly understanding. Their thoughts occur at an indescribable speed, even faster than human thought. Without distortion of any kind, their thoughts are pure, without contradiction, with perfect clarity, and express only holiness. As lightning crosses the firmament, so too do angelic thoughts pass through my mind.

I clearly perceive the difference between human thought and thought from the Wisdom of Heaven, due to the way I experience each. Thoughts from Heaven feel like light and breath; they are full of certainty, can never be forgotten, and they bring a great "amount" of truth in the blink of an eye. In an instant I understand the full meaning of each manifestation that comes to me.

Humility, prudence, and simplicity are central features of the angels. Their greatest joy is to serve God by being servants of all creation. They love human beings, animals, plants, stones, the elements, and every material and immaterial aspect of creation with a love and tenderness that, when experienced, is capable of melting even the hardest heart.

While the beauty and magnanimity of angelic visions are indescribable, they are a pale flash compared to the magnificence of those of Jesus and Mary. Nothing in the universe resembles the eternal, unnamable beauty of the hearts of Jesus and Mary. They are God made man and woman. They are the joy of the angels and have the veneration of creation. From them springs all harmony, greatness, and holiness.

The looks of Jesus and Mary, radiating such tenderness and love, melt the entire universe. Their smiles are purity itself. In their presence the soul is entranced in an ecstasy of veneration and contemplation, leaving it speechless. The soul exhales a moan of joy that says something like Ah! For me personally, contemplating the looks and smiles of Jesus and Mary is Heaven.

I hope you can understand what I'm trying to say as I try to describe the indescribable. I only say what I see, hear, and experience. Heaven exists, God exists, and God is love. This is what was given to me to see, hear, and understand.

I hope with all my heart that those who receive this manifestation let themselves be the beloved of God, more and more every day; and in this way be transformed by the beauty of a love that has no beginning nor end.

With love in Christ,

Sebastián Blaksley,
A Soul in Love
Buenos Aires, Argentina
January, 2019 and October, 2020

Prelude

A message from the Voice of Christ through a choir of Angels, in the presence of Archangel Raphael and Archangel Gabriel

The waters of life have come together. The torrents of beautiful love have merged. A new being has been recognized. A new life has been consecrated to truth. The birds of the sky sing. Joy reigns in creation. The lover and beloved have joined in the beauty of holiness. Purity has been exalted with honest truth and the recognition of love.

The lover has arrived on the shoulders of the beloved. Life has arrived and eternal truth re-vealed, written in the world so all who wish to see can follow it. The soul has reached the threshold of expressing its true identity.

Soul, you have arrived. Before time began, I conceived you in my heart to be the beauty of my being. Before the wind could blow—since movement of matter had not yet been created—you were in my divine mind as a perpetual lover. My joy was to wait for this time, a time like no other, to come, a time when the light of glory would begin to shine as never before, through you, my soul in love, my divine child.

What many-colored beauty emanates from your being! You beautify Earth and Heaven, bring-ing color to life, like waves that flow from the center of your heart. Together we are the unity of being, extending throughout the universe, bringing life to every-thing we touch, like tongues of fire that warm but do not burn, flames of holy love that sprout from your being to awaken hearts to love unceasingly.

A choir of angels surrounds you and stays united with you, child of love.

A new creation is being born in this holy place in which everything has given way to the freedom and power of love's expression: a power like no other; the force that sustains existence; reality as visible as the mountains and the flowers that embellish the Earth and from whose power they arise; a power capable of creating as much diversity as the countless ways of life across the oceans, and of stars that float serenely in universal space, resting forever in the benevolence of reality.

Every expression that will arise from you now will be united with me because of our divine un-ion. There is no need to clarify who it is who reveals this truth to you. Now you know what your true being is: always united to love, always united to the source of eternal life.

Now the world will know you in all your glory. Your voice will be heard even in the small spaces of the universe. There will be no place that does not receive the echo of the melody of our heart. Blessed soul, be the holy purity of Christ come true. You are a blessing to the world. You are a light to the nations.

A voice, so long silenced, will begin to speak with increasing force and security. Nothing will be hidden anymore. The beauty of the treasures of our heart, united in holiness, will be exposed to light so that those who walk in the world thirsty for love and truth can drink of them.

The delights of our holy love will be given to all. Thus, those who are most called to love can enjoy our beauty, and join our song of praise and gratitude.

To give ourselves entirely will be the hallmark of our expression, serving love, the joyful fruit of our union. By virtue of this, the world will have a new light. Those who seek comfort will find it. Those who long for truth will receive it. Those who grope for love will stop looking, for because of our divine union, they will recognize that love is what they are, and that their being goes wherever they go.

The time of truth has come.

1.

New Melodies of Love

A message from Jesus, identifying himself as "the living Christ who lives in you"

I. A Clear Sky

Blessed soul, beauty of eternal life! Here we are, united in a time and place that has merged into the eternal. Together we are the light of the world. United we are the sun of life. From our relationship of pure love, a new reality has been born, a reality pure and holy. We are one mind, one heart, one holy being. In our unity we are as we have always been— the immutability of being, expressing itself forever in glory.

We have arrived together at this sacred point, a point without beginning or end, where the universe and all creation that emanated from my divinity converge because of our holy love. We have reached the peak of holiness. Nothing and no one can exceed in height the elevation of this blessed place where we have arrived, holding hands, hearts melting, having entered the abode of being.

Let us be silent for a moment. Leave your sandals behind. Be barefoot. The wind of a new life blows, a breath of love renewing the face of the Earth. Come as the soul that you are, always open to discover the wondrous creations of your Mother-Father, the blessed gifts that love gives in every moment. Come ready to receive. Come willing to give. Come ready to serve.

I brought you to this port of departure through the invisible threads of my divinity, golden threads of purity, love, and truth that are felt but not seen. The breath of my Divine Love has moved your boat from the waters of oblivion to the serene currents of living water in which we now sail together in joy and peace.

You have arrived at a time in your life more magnificent than you can imagine. Neither the world's greatest treasures nor the majesties of creation can be compared to what is being created here as the fruit of our union. You have reached the abode of being.

A new song has been born in Heaven, a new light shines in the universe, a new melody of love is sung by the angels of God. It is the hymn of joy for your arrival at the portal of the path of being, a road without equal, a road that awaited your arrival as much as a mother looks forward to the birth of her beloved child.

There is no room for madness here, nor for the tempest of rough seas. Here there is only life, peace, and creation. Nothing will disturb your mind or heart anymore, since everything that afflicted your soul has been forgotten forever, erased from the memory of your heart in love. Now there will only be expressions of being, extensions of love, and unlimited giving serving the cause and effect of love.

Beloved, you have come to the land of Heaven. Tell me: what other purpose could the way of being have but to serve love?

I reveal the divine beloved. How much joy my heart feels to know that we will enjoy together, in unity with all, the free expression of your being! How much joy is in the sweet recognition of the beauty that you are, and in your free determination to live forever immersed in this truth that set you free. Truly, truly,

I tell you, to contemplate the most beautiful of sunsets is a pale flash compared to the beauty of the sky of your holy being.

Oh, joy of souls who have returned to truth, who sing new melodies of love incessantly. Their music beautifies Heaven and Earth with songs of praise to life. They live happily in the arms of their beloved. They beam sweetness in their path and their purity of heart emanates from their reality. They are living expressions of love.

Child of the wind and the sun, delight of my heart! Remember now that the being that you really are is what every truth-seeker has been looking for and that for which every lover yearning for eternal love longed. The desired unity was union with your being, a union between you and me in which we both merge into an "us" that extends the reality of love.

Here is only truth with no room for illusion. Here is creation. Here is an expression of purity and holiness. Here is reality. Here you and I live intertwined by the invisible thread of perfect love. There is no longer room for the temptations that one day led my beloved to think that she had to focus her life on survival, recognition of others, acceptance of peers, life plans—things that had nothing to do with the blessed expression of her being. All that is far behind, beyond memory.

Now the road is clear. The cloudless sky is revealed in all its beauty, your mind cleared of everything not true about yourself.

Now your mind is in a position to receive truth and accept it in perfect unity with your heart. There is no resistance any more, only the joy of being. My powerful desire is to express a love not of the world but of a heart that lives in love, in love with love, in love with Christ. A loving heart burning with the perennial desire of union.

Now this desire has become a flame that emanates from the very center of the being that you really are, the same flame with which life has been created and is sustained. It is the fire of God, burning endlessly in hearts at the center of creation, a holy fire that gives warmth to the being and extends its sweetness to everything surrounding it.

II. The Music of the Heart

L isten now to the song of the lover and the beloved. Hear how from our union arise hymns of praise and gratitude, melodies of Heaven sung in the heart given to the ardor of creative love. This music of the soul is available to all. New notes are discovered, new tones expressed, new colors painted. The novelty of unique expressions of your being become increasingly visible, even to the senses of the physical body.

Your humanity is now a divine explosion, a being expressing holiness. What other purpose can love have, but to extend itself eternally?

What a joy it is to be certain. How much joy abides in our heart! We sing with immense gratitude for having reached the path that allows an unequivocal sense of happiness as well as a deep and sincere certainty of purpose.

Bliss, fullness, and meaning: these are the three sisters who will accompany us forever as a most holy trinity. Many hearts will be attracted to beautiful love upon hearing our song. They will recognize in our expression the sweetness of love, the intensity of the fire of our union. Whoever looks at us will be captivated by the memory that resides in their most pure souls, the memory of first love, the love of the Creator.

You, blessed souls who receive the warmth of our union, recognize that in union with the love that I am in truth resides your happiness and fulfillment. You who gracefully receive these words of the divine beloved, know and accept that you are the souls most called to love. This is a gift and a mission.

Like pure flowers you have come into the world to beautify the garden of the beloved. You know love. Your heart has been wounded. You have cried in the absence of beauty and holiness. You have tirelessly sought for love that would give you security in an insecure world. Against all odds you fought to follow your destiny, and not follow who others say you should be. Do you think all of this is by chance? You know otherwise.

Dear blessed recipients of these words, your way of feeling and being is the means by which my Sacred Heart, in union with the Immaculate Heart of Mary, will be expressed on Earth, opening a portal of pure light and truth. You are an open channel to Heaven through which the flow of Divine Love will enter with increasing luminosity and create a new reality. All will occur through your free expression of the holiness you truly are. You know how to love passionately. You know where love resides. Your hearts are as sweet as honey and as powerful as a lion's roar.

Dear souls that have chosen only love, to each of you I address my words of eternal life. From Heaven I write through this helping hand to tell you in this particular way how much I love you, how beautiful your hearts are, and how much joy you give my being. You are the delight of my divinity. In your holy minds and your loving hearts I find my contentment, nested forever in my holy abode.

Dear hearts of love, joy of Heaven, passion of life, you are the salvation of the world. You are the hope that does not disappoint. You are the guarantee of the Second Coming of Christ, for I live only in hearts consumed in Divine Love. I also live in hearts that rejoice in the ability to love and be loved, hearts that smile even in the midst of the world's challenges, because at the center of their being they recognize that love lives in them. They have ignited in the fire of beautiful love.

My abode also arises in those who have made truth their only reality, those who have accepted that they are holy, beautiful, perfect, and eternally innocent. They are a gift from Heaven to Earth. They are the treasures of my Divine Love, brought into the world so it knows the beauty of God's love, a love that has no opposite.

You who receive these words, realize that you have a mission without equal. Your function now is to bring your sisters and brothers to this place you have reached—the place where the free expression of the power of the love that you really are manifests in all its glory. A place of pure expression. A place where everyone will be what they really are, and express that truth. A place of freedom and tenderness. A place of breadth. A place of holy acceptance and inclusion. A place of endless joy.

Can you begin to imagine how many beautiful pictures will now be painted? New paintings, full of beauty and purity? Can you begin to imagine the beauty of the new melodies of love that will be intoned through love's power to create music? Start now to savor the poems with which new poets will beautify the world. New expressions, never before seen, will become visible to everyone.

We enter a time like no other for humanity, a time of love's power freely expressed. A time marked by freedom, freedom that will manifest itself in very concrete expressions full of love and kindness. You who have arrived first among many to this place, be aware of what you are being told. Your path home has been long. You have reached your purpose in the world.

Your arrival is the perfect way to become aware of what you are. Your being was created by love alone. It is an extension of holiness. It is a perfect expression of truth. There is no homework, no mission to accomplish, no obligations or plans of any kind.

You are not looking for anything. You do not need anything. You need not give anything. You simply are. And because you simply are, you have an inherent impulse to express yourself freely in harmony with what you are. That driving force of being leads you to create in new ways, always beautifully, always authentically. This is why no higher path can be traveled than this path of being: a path where what you really are is fully manifested.

Since what you are has been established by God from all eternity, only through the union of your heart with the divine heart can you be yourself in spirit and in truth. Only in the love that comes from God, the essence of your being and of everything that exists, can you truly express yourself. Why? Because you are truth, love, and life. You are the way.

III. Firm Rock

The world cannot teach you to be what you really are because it cannot teach you what love is. The world teaches nothing. It never had a teaching function. The world is simply a platform where you express what you are or what you are not. It is like a great art gallery where each one of you exhibits your work. Simply that.

Would it make sense for a painter to blame the exhibition hall for his works? He painted and exhibited them himself. He could not keep from expressing himself. The urge to exhibit what emanates from oneself is too strong. Since it was better to express than not, he expressed what he could express in the way he could express. Perhaps the painter did not like the works that came from his heart, which is the source of every being. Nevertheless, they reveal how much the artist of these works loves himself in truth and holiness.

To love who you are is to love your expressions also. So if at any time in your life you believe that what came from you was unworthy of being loved, then you had not reached the fullness of love. When you return to your state of being, you can only love your being, that is, loving who you are and consequently your expression. Every expression that arises from you is worthy of being loved because of who you are, especially where you fell and where you rose, where your most enlightened frustrations and anger were born. In the realm of expression is where you encountered the obstacles you perceived as limitations.

Not being who you really are is the real tragedy, not only for you but for everyone, because every time you refuse to be and reject your expression, a light of beauty and purity is denied to all. To create a new world is to give expression to the love you are without interruption. There is no other way to create anything because, as demonstrated in this work, love is the foundation of creation. Only love creates.

Expressing and creating are the same. You are now ready to allow your being to express itself freely in union with the truth that is always true. Further, you recognize that free will has been given you. You can freely choose with me the way you will express the love that you truly are.

Is it not true that now everything makes sense? The notion that you were free to deny your being makes no sense when examined in the calm light of truth. When the mind made use of the gift of freedom, it was an improper use. Using freedom to choose not to love is an abuse of freedom that is not part of God's plan, because love cannot do anything that would deny its essence. What would be the purpose of such a crazy idea?

You have been told repeatedly that you are free, have always been and always will be. That is eternally true. However, what was not sufficiently clarified is in what sense this freedom is expressed.

True freedom consists of allowing your being to manifest freely. Expressing oneself freely is synonymous with being free. Could a free being not express itself? Obviously not, for the liberation so sought after was but liberation from everything that limited your free expression.

Yet you repressed your true self for so long that it was necessary to travel this path carefully, step by step, to bring you to this time when you are no longer bound. You have now reached the state in which you love yourself enough to be able to live from the love you really are. There are no more reasons not to be who you are, to hide what you feel and what you think.

Let us continue to weave a new fabric, the fabric of freedom. As was revealed to you, the heart is the center of your being, which is where mind, soul, and heart are in union. You were also shown that it is there where feelings are born, just as it is in the mind where thoughts are born, and that both are linked to the will that the soul possesses. Beyond all that, it has been explained to you with sweetness, patience, and wisdom that you are love, for the simple reason that you are a child of God.

Because what you are is love, your mind and heart cannot contain anything other than love. Thus your true expression of being is full of love, compassion, beauty, and holiness. What form it finally takes does not matter, for it will always be soaked with love. It will be an expression of truth because of its source.

In this work when we refer to "expression," we refer to the feelings, thoughts, desires, and movements of your heart that then take form. Therefore before a manifestation takes form, there must be a source that gives it life. There can be no beautiful music without a musician who created it; it cannot exist if you do not have music in your heart. First inside, then outside.

If you understand what is being said in this dialogue emerging from our union, you can begin to see the structure in larger perspective, and how different it is from the house built on sand. Now the holy abode shines in all its magnificence. Its beauty attracts those who seek the truth with a full heart. Its simplicity confuses the minds of those who wish to explain everything. Its holiness inspires new generations. It is an ode to life.

What a joy to know that our holy being is our only reality! What a joy to recognize sweetly that love is the only truth of our reality, no matter where we think we are and who we have believed ourselves to be. Your every expression of love bears witness to your truth. Everything that is not love is unreal. How simple! How true. How freeing.

The truth has set you free. Not only the truth that you are as God created you, but all truth.

My love, joy of my heart as a divine lover, stay by me. Let me feel your heartbeat. Rest quietly on my chest, listening to my heartbeat. Immerse yourself in the rhythmic union of our hearts. They beat as one, they move as one, indistinguishable one from the other. We are the concord of love now. We are holiness expressing. We are fullness. We are one being.

2.

The Wind Blows

A message from the Archangel Raphael

I. Profit Comes From Giving

What could be the cause of your not loving the expression of who you are but your decision not to love yourself? A being who does not love herself is in conflict with what she is, and therefore in conflict with everything, for if you disagree with who you are, you project that anger towards everything in one way or another. When not loving yourself, you try to get rid of who you are, which is impossible. Given that impossibility, once you reject who you really are—which is in itself a lack of love—you create situations in which you to deny yourself; you cannot delete yourself but you can deny it. And so, closing your eyes to your being, you are like children who hope that when they close their eyes the danger disappears, or at least that by not seeing it, the other does not see them. You either look the other way, or fear the look of love.

When speaking of the mechanism of denial, remember the childish idea that what eyes do not see, the heart does not feel. This part of the mind is afraid of the holiness of your own being. However, you have reached maturity of consciousness and no longer think or feel like a child—although you will always be like a child in the arms of love. We recall this again to become aware that the only reason for such responses is fear of the power of the expression of being.

What other reason could there be to fear the power that manifests your being? Consider this carefully, for in your answer lies either your complete liberation or your captivity in non-expression. Be silent for a moment. Let the wisdom of being give you the answer. Let love prepare you for revelation.

You fear the power of the expression of love because you believe that the manifestation of your being could somehow destroy, or invoke an attack. You have so much love for your true being that you have tried to hide it from the eyes of others, hide it from the world. And so you would protect it as you would a priceless treasure which you are unwilling to risk. That was how you historically responded to love.

How you respond to who you are is directly related to your idea of yourself. For you to consider yourself unworthy, you had to have seen within yourself something that, according to your interpretation, was not loving or not worthy of being loved. That was the problem. While no longer the case, we still must openly acknowledge that when you denied your being, you denied your expression.

A mind reconciled with itself and a heart living in peace are the twin pillars upon which the abode of the light that you really are is built, and within which love expresses itself in all its beauty. Every being expresses through the mere fact of its existence, so when you reconcile with what you are, you extend peace. And where peace is, there love is also.

It is insufficient merely to recognize that you are perfect love, or that your being lives in peace within the embrace of holiness. Rather it is necessary that this reality be manifested, for being and the expression of being are undivided. Indeed, separation itself was nothing more than a disunity between being and its expression.

That you have always been and will be holy is beyond question. Your being was created by God, who only creates holiness, beauty, and perfection. But that you have consciously expressed that truth in the world is not so obvious to you, although it is for God. I will clarify.

You thought it possible to express either love or its opposite, but you did not stop to think about how impossible such a belief is. Within the reality of being there are no such distinctions. Either you are or you are not. There is no third option. And because, once created, you are eternal and cannot stop being what you are, you have always been extending the being you really are. Always. You have always been extending love.

You have extended yourself as much as God has, for you are God's extension. No expression of Divine Love can stop creating new love. And as an extension of the being that God is, you have created love in union with Christ. Be aware of this; recognize this truth, for it is one thing to realize something, and another thing altogether to recognize that what you realize is part of you. To recognize the love you have extended from your true being is to recognize the truth about yourself. It is to recognize your holy, perfect, beautiful creations. They are the creations that God constantly births through your being. They are part of you as much as you are part of God. To accept them as well-loved children, born from the center of your heart in love, in perfect union with Christ, is to love yourself in the expression of who you really are.

II. Life and Expression

The full picture can now be seen. If you cancel the expression of what you are, you cancel the true being from which it emerges. Obviously this does not mean that the being ceases to exist, but that its lack of expression prevents your consciousness from noticing its existence. This prevents you from being able to meet yourself. And if you don't fully meet yourself, you cannot live in the fullness of being—which is the same as saying you are not. Remember, being expresses itself to make itself known. This is how it participates in existence, or knowledge, for knowing and being are linked.

The expression of being is its creation. In fact, God's creations, among which you find yourself, are God's expressions. Divine creations cannot be sinful, imperfect, or horrifying; if they were, God would have to be that way. Expression is to being as breath is to the life of the body.

A writer improves continuously as she reads and writes. Sometimes she can later incorporate something that she has read as part of her writing, be it the tone or content. As she writes, she becomes more skillful. The same goes for a painter or a musician. They grow in their capacity to the extent that they put their art into practice and observe similar artistic expressions.

In the case of the writer, the relationship that exists between what she reads and what she writes is one of receiving and giving, an inseparable continuum if the author wishes to grow and discover new, increasingly subtle and exquisite ways of expressing what she wishes with words. Writing and reading are part of a whole. The same goes for being and expression; they are an inseparable part of your wholeness, your totality.

When you express who you really are, you grow. By joining others who express what they really are, you also grow, just as a writer grows by reading new works and continuing to write. Just as you grow in the knowledge of your being by expressing yourself, and you receive inspiration from other expressions of truth, the same goes for your sisters and brothers in relation to you.

When you extend the love you are, others who also seek to express the truth of their being join you. From this union they get the strength to be more authentic in their expressions. Thus you act as a source of inspiration for others to dare to fly. When you see them, fly to them and to others who are undertaking the flight of spirit. In this way you encourage yourself to fly higher and higher. This flow of inspiration, received and given, constitutes a force of union in holiness, true communion in eternal extension, always growing, always new.

Both being and its expression are eternal. The need for expression of being is limitless. You will always find new ways to manifest, to make yourself known. As you absorb inspiration from the expressions of other similar beings, you grow in your ability to express. In this way being widens more and more in a movement of endless expansion.

Can you glimpse the relationship that exists between freedom of expression and limitless being? When we spoke of the unconditionality of love, we were speaking of the unconditionality of being. This does not mean you must love everyone without limit; if you feel that you do not love or like someone, you need not pretend. This unconditionality does not concern the limits of the body, or anything related to time or space. When we talked about unconditional being, we spoke of being without limit to its expression. This is what you have always been. You have no limits. Nothing and no one can limit your expression— not even you. You are always manifesting in one way or another.

Only in love can you express who you really are, because your being is one of pure love, and outside of love is nothing.

In nothing there is no expression. We can now understand the significance of everything from the perspective of being.

We said that sin is a lack of love. We can understand now that it is a lack of expression of being. In other words, sin is the deliberate decision to prevent love from expressing itself. This deliberate decision is a determination not to share the being you are. The negation of an expression of love is the essence of self-ishness. To withhold an expression of the love you really are is to shortchange yourself.

When you skimp on the expression of your true being, you skimp on love, and your consciousness is clouded. That was why you once plunged into fear—a fear of expressing yourself, a fear of extending the love of your being. That fear arose from the decision not to give of yourself. By doing that, you lost sight of the fullness of your being, which is attained by giving yourself.

III. Give Yourself the Fullness of Being

It was said that the seal of the way of being would be giving. Giving is what a being needs to do because a being who does not give himself cannot live fully, for he is not full. A decision not to share the your authentic being leads to a loss of the awareness of your fullness. And since what exists in consciousness is all that is true, if the fullness of your being is not in your consciousness, you will feel less than full and will live as such. That will create an inner state of great tension. Being will prod you to let itself be.

You have often prevented your freedom of expression. I am not referring to times when you decided, in union with love and reason, not to manifest something that you felt or thought. Nor am I referring to the times when you were silent for love. I am referring to your inner world, the times when you did not allow yourself to feel what you felt or think what you thought. And you censored others, silently or out loud.

With this observation we are not bringing the past to the present, for doing so makes no sense. Trying to bring illusion to reality is no longer an active mental mechanism for you. What we are doing is removing past emotions so you can integrate all experience in the reality of love.

Censorship is as foreign to love as illusion is to truth. God does not censor or limit expression. Everyone has the right to think as they want to think and feel as they want to feel. Like a wise Father, God shows the law of cause and effect, so through reason you can discern, either in advance or through experience. However you access the truth, you know it exists and that it is one with your being.

The ability to discern is an inherent characteristic of the human spirit, an ability given at creation. Everyone knows there is a good that is always good, a truth that is always true, a love that is true love. You were born with that knowledge as part of your essence. Your feelings testify that this is true. With a given action, you feel either peaceful or restless.

The range of emotions from one extreme to the other form an authentic color palette that tells you how close you are to love, or how far away, in different gradations.

Remember that the life of your soul is characterized by a simple truth: you are within the heart of God. The question is how united to love you live. It is all about union. Either you are completely united to Christ or not. Either you maintain a relationship with love in which it is everything to you, or in which it is nothing to you, with endless options, grades, or nuances in between.

A reconciled being is the necessary condition for you to be able to join love, to freely be the love you are without creating a substitute identity.

Let us play the game of beautiful truth a little. Imagine your soul as if it were located on a straight line. In the center of the line is the zero point. If you move to the right, you are getting closer and closer to love. Going to the left moves farther away from it. The zero point is where we are now, the gateway to this path of being. It is the point to which perfect forgiveness has taken you—a point in which the mind has reconciled with what it is, and therefore has been stripped of guilt.

The mind has been freed from fear, and having been freed, it flew to the truth, making it one with the heart. By joining with the heart, the mind is reinstated to reason. With that, your being recognizes itself for what it is: reconciled. Not because it needs to reconcile with anything or anyone, because it was never in conflict, but because the mind has seen everything through the eyes of truth. Once united with the heart, the mind looks upon all through the eyes of love. With this soul vision, what you are shines with the glory of perfect innocence. Your being has recovered its two wings, so to speak: love and reason. Now your true being begins to fly.

From this moment on you no longer walk, but fly. Your expressions will flow as freely as the wind. Increasingly you will witness the speed of mind and heart. You will move faster than lightning—that is how free your mind will be. Such will be the force of inspiration which arises from spirit and manifests itself through thought. In other words, you will no longer think anything. You will simply enjoy being. You will simply flow and be carried in a firm, accurate, sweet way by the swell formed by the force that arises from the union of truth and love, the union of your thoughts and feelings.

Your imagination will activate as never before. You will see new images. New ideas will be born in your mind from which light, certainty, and beauty emanate. You will see new universes full of love. Creativity will express as beautifully as a flower and as tenderly as a firefly. It will have the force of water, which, while soft and harmless, is also capable of shaping everything in its path. This will be your expression from now on: the pure movement of love and freedom.

You will sing new songs. You will create a space in which the being can expand to its full breadth. You will experience the long-awaited freedom to be who you really are. Because of your union with the love you are, liberty will be born in you. New worlds will arise from within—the truth will be evident in each petal of every flower, in each wing of every bird in the sky, in each star, and also in each of your sisters and brothers who, moved by their desire to respond to the call of love, will join us in spirit and truth. Together, they, we, Christ, and you, fused in the same love, will create a kingdom within the Kingdom of Heaven.

United, perfection will extend to include everyone. No one will be excluded. The wind of our spirit of love and truth will blow and move consciousness toward love. Not everyone will join our flight. But those who do will find in our creations an unknown "something" that calls them to join. They will be blessed by the divine relationship that our union manifests. And it will fly, moved by the breath of purity and holiness that emanates from the love in our hearts. Together we will continue to spread beautiful love for all eternity, living forever in the solace of God's peace.

3.

Divine Whispers

A message from Mother Mary

I. The Treasure of Creating Love

My child,
Listen to the voice of the beloved of your soul.
Stay in the sweetness of its song.
Immerse yourself in the depths of its beauty.
Think, soul in love: What will the flowers hear so that they
open in gratitude and beautify life?
What do the waters listen to so that they begin to dance
with joy?
What does love whisper to the human heart so that it can
love even God?
Every morning life is reborn.
Every moment, the whisper of love is heard in the creatures.
Everyone has a heart.
The melodies of creation are awakened.
Everything sings happily. Created beings rise to bear
witness to love.
Each day corresponds to its melody, a melody of love
and truth.

Listen to the music of your heart. Watch how everything
  praises love.
Colors beautify the gardens.
The saints of holiness express their joy and give thanks for
  having been called to life.
The banquet is served.
The beloved calls everyone to sit at the table, to enjoy the
  delights of creating the holy, the beautiful, the perfect.
Rejoice in your glory. It is the glory of the Mother.

With these plain words of love and sweetness I give you your treasure. In it resides the blessed gift of eternal life. Receive it. I give it to you with all my love. I give it to you with my immaculate hands, full of purity and holiness. It is the treasure that remained hidden in the depths of the heart of God, so that it may be given to you on the day it was written. Divine custody has kept it for you.

Child of truth, beauty of God, I give you my love, I give you my being, I give it to be yours forever.

Now your consciousness will accept in a greater and joyful degree the reality of our union, the truth of your holy being. Remember that my being belongs to you, just as you belong to me.

Receive the present of your inheritance. Receive the gift of your being. It is God's present for you.

My love, child of my bosom, joy of the Mother of the living! A love that is not of the world is given you. A truth that comes from Heaven is revealed. New life is born in you. You are new, forever renewed in the spirit of God.

Let us sing new songs together. Let us dance as did King David, but with the beauty of our uniqueness.

Rise up, beloved of God! Move with the dance of life! Look, many are coming. They are our beloved brothers and sisters who come to hear the melodies that flow from our union. Together the beloveds are a refuge of holy love, the abode where others will come to drink the waters of life. They are unity expressed on Earth.

The Earth has heard the truth. Pure spirits move upon hearing the voice of our union. Enlightened souls sing along with those who seek the light. Hearts vibrate in love.

New flowers are born every day. The sun always shines. The trees sway to the rhythm of the wind, cheerfully dancing to the song of beautiful love.

The beloved whispers to the always-loved ones of the Creator. Rejoicing in life, She expresses Her love in an explosion of endless diversity. It is the response of the created to the Creator. It is an undulating movement of giving and receiving lived in an ecstasy of love.

Blessed soul! Your being has been protected for so long! God kept it inviolable. For all eternity you remained in God, waiting for the perfect moment when your conscious acceptance made it possible to be given and received jubilantly.

You already know the whisper of love which sweetly calls to your ear every night and every morning. You know what the voice says: it calls you to the bed of love and truth.

II. A New Revelation

Loving heart! Let the song of the birds fill the abode of your being. Become one with the wind. Rest in the grace of contemplation. Rest in the benevolence of the universe. Life flows in abundance where you are, because you are life in fullness. The river of the abundance of your being overflows, and in its vital exuberance creates new life. Create love wherever you are. Where sweetness dwells, there dwells your truth. Where the waters are born, there you are, and where they flow is eternity.

We are the source of eternal life. We are the unity of being. We are the concord of the world. Holy creation, blessed love, sweetness of the aromas of the most exquisite spring flowers, happiness of living, bliss of being, our song is our gift to our Beloved. It is the response of our love to the One who gives life. We open our arms to embrace the world. We welcome all who wish to sing a new song, the song of beautiful love. We call everyone to our union. We bless who we are. We sanctify what joins our being of pure holiness. United we are the immaculate conception, extending without limit. We are the perfect expression of God's love.

A new melody is heard and resonates in your heart, the song of Mary, a song that the Mother sings with her child, a hymn as melodious as the most beautiful symphonies of the angels of Heaven. In this orchestra of full life—the creation of the three times holy—we are a harp with sustained notes of love and truth, sounds of beauty and holiness.

Our singing will be heard to the ends of the Earth. The stars will shine brighter because of it. The sun will shine with greater clarity and benevolence on the meadows. Marigolds will greet this love with bright, new, serene colors. New lives will be created in union with this song of the soul in love, a new song of love and truth, the song of life.

Roses open to receive the sun of love. Winds move to give life to everything. Everything is in perfect cadence with divine music. All dance to the rhythm of truth.

Today is the day of days, the perfect moment in which you receive your being. Accept it with joy and serenity.

Child of light, I reveal to you a great truth. Please listen.

When you were created, you were called to exercise your free will. In your essence there is the cry of freedom. Your Creator always knew that, first of all, He should create a reality where freedom exists. So He guarded your holy being until you could make the choice for love. It was buried like a seed in damp soil, waiting for the perfect time to germinate. That moment has arrived. That moment is now.

Your being was locked securely within the heart of Christ, to be given to you when you yourself claimed your inheritance. That treasure is literally God's plan for you. It is the divine will come true for your being. It could not be delivered before this moment; you were not ready. But now you are, and so I give it to you. Love placed it in my immaculate hands and honored me with the gift of giving it to you, and with it, new life.

All beings called into existence receive the gift of life arising from the pure love that God is. But not everyone receives the treasure I speak of here. This blessed treasure, which with love I give you today, is the treasure of being a reliable expression of God's love in a degree of union between the Creator and the created. Not all beings can receive; not all have been created for it, although all beings are complete to the degree that they can accept.

In a sense, each heart is like a beautiful goblet. Each is a different size, which love calls to fill with its waters. The hearts are not filled arbitrarily, even if they are thirsty. To be filled, they must want to be filled. Longing is always fulfilled. Love always recognizes the voice of the beloved and responds to the call of the heart. Divine Love never lacks reciprocity.

God Herself conceived the human spirit and imbued it with the ability to absorb divinity. Humans were given the power to be the children of the Highest. Power is not given to all beings, nor is it necessary. God loves diversity.

What is happening today, here and now, is that the treasure of being a conscious expression of God's love is given to you forever, and with it, union with God. You had not received it before but now you have. It is here. It is yours. Honor it. You asked. Heaven answered.

The treasure is not itself an identity, although it cannot be active without one. Nor is it unity itself. The union of human nature with the divine is a prerequisite. Nor is it about remaining in unity with God, since everything that exists lives in God. For the treasure to be, there must be something new in the human spirit. That "something" is what makes the spirit's existence meaningful.

Every being exists for a reason. This treasure makes sense of your creation. It is the purpose of your reality. What is this that I call the "treasure of your being"? What is it that you receive today with all my love?

It is the ability to participate in the glory of the Mother in all Her extensions, length, and breadth without limits of any kind and thus to be aware of all that God is aware of. It enables you to look at everything through the eyes of Christ, to participate fully in the processes of love.

Through this "ability" to merge with the divine essence, to be God in God, you are unique in all creation. In short, this treasure is the divine uniqueness that you are. You might argue that all beings are unique, and in that you are correct. That the human being is different from all other beings is beyond question. Just by comparing humanity to other creations that inhabit the Earth, it is clear that there is something in humanity that is not in the others. There is a reason why Christ made himself present as a man and not another creature.

Here I am not comparing differences in form, but those at a deeper level. For example, if you look at animals, you will see that each is similar to the other in their nature. The same is true with plants. All are born, grow, some multiply, and then their bodies cease to be in time and space as they had been. Their existence is based exclusively on survival. In this there is no difference between any living being on Earth except humankind.

Humankind creates culture, sings songs, conceives complex societies, shapes the Earth, brings together the elements in multiple ways, and gives rise to new constellations of reality, as with technology, laws, or forms of government. All this is not always associated with mere survival.

Humankind is the only species on Earth who can build majestic cathedrals, or paint works of art that connect memories of beauty and the sublime. Only humankind is capable of building health centers to heal bodies and minds. Humanity carries the seed of solidarity and love of neighbor, as no other earthly being can. Humankind has the ability to raise thoughts and feelings to such high levels that there is no difference between their way of being and that of the Creator. Humankind is aware of love and being, and is touched by the love of God as no other being can be: responding to love as only humanity can.

III. Always Create a New Love

What is it about human beings who have fallen in love with God? What has love whispered to the human heart that, when accepted, allows it to become God in God? What does the divine heart hold for the joy of humanity? What is the Creator's plan?

Here, in a way that has not been done before, we are approaching the essence of the truth of your being, the treasure of your existence. Start feeling into these questions. Become aware of what they mean. Feel the answer without trying to put it into words. Just observe what surrounds you without judging anything, and think with me once more: what makes humankind like this?

Accept the beauty of human nature. Let yourself be dazzled by the thresholds of knowledge which humanity is capable of reaching. Marvel at the greatness of that being that God loves so much, and in whom God has put all Her predilection.

Beloved children! Blessed humanity! You are being given a great revelation which shows that your spirits carry within them the seeds of the divine beyond that of any other created being. You, in union, can access the greatest degree that can be achieved, since you can truly join your source consciously; and through that capacity eternally create new expressions of love. No other creature can do so, even though they are all extensions of divine beauty.

God loves all creations. However, not all merge in Her. Only those that have been destined for it from all eternity can do so in the perfect wisdom of the Creator. You are among them, particularly you who receive these words full of the power of Heaven.

That to which you are always called by the will of God contains the treasure now being given. You were created to be the conscious light of love's glory. You were created to merge in God. To become nothing in Divine Love. No separated mind can understand the greatness of this gift. But the heart in love understands and is open to this gift even when it greatly exceeds all that the beloved could imagine or desire.

God's design for you is great, as big as the universe and greater. Let yourself be carried away by its greatness. Do not fear the height of holiness. Remember, you are never more than when you merge in love.

What God whispered to your heart at the moment of your creation, and continues to whisper in every moment, is something that no one and nothing can know until you manifest it yourself. That whisper of beautiful love you will now begin to extend without limit with your expression of its voice, its content, and its quality.

Creation now asks you, who have chosen only love: What has love whispered to you? Tell all. The universe implores you, lovingly, out of the sanctity of the Creator's being. Everyone wants to hear. Tell of the delights of beautiful love that only the beloved can give.

Share, beloved of Christ, the melodies that your divine beloved sings to you, for if you withhold, a star goes out and a nightingale stops singing. Let everyone know the beauty of the divine whisper, the tenderness of love without beginning or end that caresses your soul like nothing else.

4.

The Testimony of the Truth

A message from Jesus, identifying himself as the Living Christ who lives in you

I. The Mirror of the Creator

The path of being is one of immense responsibility in which you commit yourself to follow forever what your being dictates through your heart and mind united in holiness. This responsibility demands no effort, nor is it a burden. What is necessary is to assume the responsibility of respecting, honoring, and showering yourself with love, and above all taking care of that very pure child given to you, the treasure of pure love that you really are.

For as long as you walked the path of life you have been vacillating between your wishes and needs, your thoughts and feelings, doing what others told you to do and what you wanted to do, and both options ended up being pretty much more of the same. None of this is what we speak of now, for to guide your life on the basis of desires that come from an emotional-mental construct, formed by the family, societal, or cultural mandates of the world, is to follow what has nothing in spirit and truth to do with your being.

It is important to recognize that your being never was nor will be part of anything alien to truth, the purpose of its existence. God created your being, and did not do so for passing or insignificant matters. He created you to be the perfect manifestation of the light of His glory, and thus literally to know Himself.

Creation reflects its Creator, and your works reflect you. Creations are the mirror of their creator. Thus they see themselves reflected and know each other. By their fruits are they known.

Look at your world—not another's, yours. Observe calmly. Contemplate it through the eyes of love. What have you done with your life? I refer not to the events themselves, but to your response to events. What emerged reflects the options you exercised in every moment.

You may still feel you don't like things in your life, wish things were different, or wish you hadn't existed at all. I know every movement of your heart even feelings that are now a distant memory, almost nonexistent. Because this is true, I can use them for my purpose now.

I know very well that the past has no power over you, and that you have already accepted this eternal truth. The past happened. What a joy now to live in the eternal present of love. Therefore it is unnecessary to become entangled in analysis. I do not advocate the thinking mind as a source of wisdom; that stage has been left behind.

What I am speaking of now is the way of being and its expression. Everyone has a feeling about things they don't like in some aspect of their lives, or in the world. That feeling is simply an interpretation of specific elements of life, those elements that arouse anger, without considering the whole. If you could accept them simply as expressions of what you thought you were rather than as expressions of your true self, you would begin to forgive your manifestations and cease to feel angry. This is really forgiving yourself, loving yourself sincerely.

II. Love Your Expressions

In actuality you did not blame the world for your supposedly unfortunate life or for its cruelty. You blamed yourself. That was the basis of the heartbreak and anger you felt. If you do not like the work you have hung in the exhibition, it is because you have judged it instead of understanding it for what it is: a manifestation that serves you to know yourself which will lead you serenely along the path of life.

You have been told that life is created in every moment. It is not static. Therefore you are reborn with each day break, and again with each sunset, and continue being reborn each night surrounded by stars and sacred silence. No moment is the same as any another. Therefore if you do not like the expressions that emerge from your life you now can use discernment differently than you could previously.

Discernment was not given for you to be a ruthless or reckless judge. Its purpose is for you to see clearly what expresses love and what does not, so you can consciously choose what you want.

With true discernment you could never do anything contrary to love; you would know what love is and that only love can make you happy and allow you to live in the fullness of being. Only love is holiness. Only love is truth. Only love is union. You know all this because you know yourself perfectly well. In the past you may have used childish methods to try to convince yourself, the world, and God that you didn't know your true self. That attempt may have become an obsession. You may have been convinced it was true. Now, however, you are beyond the stage of immature denial, or a consciousness other than of the greatness of your being. You have been released from all that hindered the glow of truth in your mind.

Your greatness is far above anything that can be weighed, valued, imagined, or defined. Your greatness was eternally decreed by your Creator from the very moment of your creation.

If you do not like your expressions, change your mentality. Observe your heart and discard from it whatever is not love. You will see how your new expressions change. Your heart will rejoice and your mind will rest in peace. You are an eternal creator extending in every moment. Every word you utter arises from your heart. Every thought you think comes from your mind. Every decision you make is based on what you believe and what you think you are. We reiterate this because of its importance.

One reason there may have been a time in the past when you were not responsible for your actions or your expressions is that you perceived them as being automatic. The true importance of this must be explained.

Please lovingly consider the following. If you are with someone and you start to say things you did not intend to say, or fall into unexplainable exaggerations or otherwise are in situations in which you do things without knowing why you did them—then in a moment of reflection, you wonder, how could I have said or done such a thing? And you have the feeling that it was not really you who did that, or maybe you are not who you thought you were, since who you had thought you were could not have done or said those things. Although such experiences are not powerful any longer, if the old impulsivity is still there, we will now remove it.

When your expressions do not faithfully reflect your real feelings or thoughts, you are expressing unconsciousness. Only in that sense are those expressions yours. Either you consciously or unconsciously express the truth of who you are. Now you have true discernment about who you are, and therefore who your brother or sister is as well. To disconnect from the truth of who you are is to disconnect from your true feelings and thoughts, which are always loving and truthful. Every true expression is an expression of love.

III. The Prayer of Expression

We are speaking of the way of being. Therefore we will refer everything to the reality of the being you really are. Remember, because you exist you cannot stop expressing yourself; and everything that exists manifests in one way or another. This is the same as saying that you always communicate, and cannot not communicate. Expression of being is communication. Expression is a message you launch into the world that says:

Brothers and sisters, look at me; this is what I think I am.

This prayer that you release to the universe through the expression of your being must be understood in both of its two parts. First you say, "Look at me." That is, you seek to be known and not ignored. In this there is no conflict. It arises from the desire to know that you exist and to be known. Upon realizing your existence in creation, you can know that you exist, otherwise you would live in ignorance of yourself.

The second part of the prayer says, "This is what I think I am." The second aspect is the problem that you have had so far concerning what you manifest, for to express yourself from a place where you "think" you are this or that is to derive the power of expression from an illusory source. If you manifest yourself according to beliefs, you are not expressing yourself in truth. This is essential to understand in order to continue weaving the new fabric of freedom.

In the realm of beliefs there is always room for conflict. Although beliefs may point to truth, truth cannot be present in beliefs. Beliefs are a signpost showing the direction of the destination, but are not the destination itself. Such simple truth this is. To cling to beliefs is but to cling to a signpost. Hugging the post prevents you from moving forward.

You can see how this matter of clinging to the signpost of beliefs is not only contrary to the truth, but is a danger. If traveling on a road you see a sign telling you to turn lest you go over a cliff, and you just stare at the signpost, the consequences may be unfortunate.

Signposts are loving messengers that make your path safe and peaceful.

You have always been, and therefore you have always expressed yourself. However, you have not always expressed yourself from this truth. In this sense we could say that if you manifest yourself from the basis of the truth of yourself, then you are being; otherwise you are nothing, since beyond truth is nothing. This is what was meant when it was said that you either are, or you are not.

You cannot stop being. However, you can express yourself either from truth or illusion. That does not change your being, but it changes your expression, and with that, the awareness you have of yourself and that others have of you. Expressing from illusion creates a flow of giving and receiving within the illusion, rather than in truth and love. In order that you can be faithful to who you really are, and have a mechanism that allows you to remain in truthful expression, God placed in your heart a feeling that makes you uncomfortable when you betray yourself. We call that feeling "the cry of being."

When you express yourself from what you think you are supposed to be, you are trying to manifest an ideal self. It brings unhappiness because it is not real. It is not what you are. Your uneasiness bears witness to it. That feeling must be honored. Listen to this inner teacher of the truth of your being.

Until you joined this path you could never manifest who you really are because of the nature of your beliefs.

It is essential to be absolutely committed to truth in order to follow the path of being, which joins the path of the heart. These paths join because the heart and the being are truly united. Together you become integrated, and from that integrity you act with true honesty.

Can you start to see how insincere it is to express yourself from what you really are not? Can you see why it is impossible to be happy if you are not really yourself every moment of your life? Can you begin to glimpse what the will of God means?

You were created to be who you really are and nothing less. When you act, feel, or think in a certain way because "others" say that things should be a certain way, and follow as others say you should be without personal reflection, you are going against the will of God.

Can you begin to realize what the world exists for? It exists for you to learn to express yourself as you really are, to learn to be yourself. That is being love.

IV. A New Holy Prayer

We said we would show you a new meaning for what you call prayer. If what you expressed before was a belief based on a worldly mental construct that could never be the truth of who you are, you now need to express yourself from the truth of being.

In your being lies the wisdom of God. Therefore, you already know what you are and how to manifest. When your being was created, it was also endowed with the innate ability to do so without effort, just as the sun makes no effort to shine.

We are talking about moving from, "This is what I think I am," to "This is what I am." In order to make this movement, it is necessary to pass through the path of knowledge, which could not be traveled before completing the path of transformation, which is integral to the path of the heart.

Only I can tell you what you really are, because I am your true being. Only in union with me can you express the love you really are because I am the love you are in spirit and truth. Consider this statement in silence. Read it again. Take it into the depths of your heart and stay with it. Make it yours. Start feeling what these words bring up in you.

Who is the one speaking these words? Who is the one receiving them? Who is replying?

If I am your being—and I assure you that I am—who are you who hears my voice?

In the answer to this question lies the essence of your true identity, and the gateway to the true expression of your being.

I am your being, I am Christ. Therefore I am you. What hears my voice is your awareness. What observes how my being is absorbed by your consciousness is the part of your mind that has the ability to be an impartial observer. It is what makes you attentive.

This is easy to understand if you look at your body. Take some distance from it now. Watch the fingers move. Is what you observe something separate from you? Those fingers that make coordinated movements with the hand and the rest of the body, are they not yours? Of course they are. Therefore what you observe, in this case your fingers and your hands, is part of you. This means that you can observe yourself totally or partially. For that to be possible, you have to have a consciousness that allows you to see what you observe. What is observed, the observer, and the consciousness that allows the observer to be aware of observing, are part of the same reality of being. Observed, observer, and awareness of observing are different aspects of the same reality.

I am, in such a way that I am what gives existence to your being. I am the creative force of life. I am the element that constitutes your being and all being. Your ability to observe me without judgment is part of you as much as your being of which I am the source and the life. The awareness that allows you to realize that you listen to me, observe, and sustain a relationship of intimate love with me, is as much yours as your being and I are.

I am the source of your being, that which makes your being what it is. I am the vital breath of your spirit, or if you prefer, your Creator. Nothing and no one can tell you what you are other than me. This is because what my divine will provides is only revealed to each particular spirit. I am not telling everyone what only you need to know. What my will provides and what your being is, are one and the same.

The relationship of intimate love between you and me, between who you are and your source, is an inviolable space. Therefore, remaining attached to me is how you really are. We are now able to reframe the prayer and replace it with a new holy prayer, united to the truth, by saying:

I am Christ, I have come into the world to bear witness to the truth. I am the way, the truth, and the life.

5.

New Forms of Love

A message from the Voice of Christ through a choir of Angels,
in the presence of Archangel Raphael and Archangel Gabriel

I. The Honesty of Being

The path of being is not about a personality trying to be. Do not be confused, for the personality is as temporary as the body. It will remain in the realm of time beyond its utility for realizing your path. Everything of time will cease to be in time; what is of eternity is eternal. This is a simple truth.

To express who you really are and not from illusion is to express the living Christ who lives in you. That is to say, perfect love. As we have said, often the anger you feel comes from the belief that your expression is autonomous, that is, that your feelings and thoughts are not your own, an old mental mechanism in which you sought not to take responsibility for your life and justified your anger by telling yourself and God that you were at the mercy of forces you could not control.

The path of being sets aside the belief that you are not responsible for what you feel, think, and experience. You assume full responsibility for your mental processes and for what your heart feels. You are also aware that you have the ability to choose. Consequently you accept the directions you have chosen and that not all of them gave you happiness, although some did. You no longer seek to convince yourself that the life you lived was wonderful and the world is a paradise, when in fact you know it is not, even though it can be transformed by love.

The difficulty of the path of being comes from the fear of truth. You believe, although perhaps not very consciously, that if you always live in truth, you will somehow be punished for a world devoid of sincerity. It does not have to be that way.

The time has passed when the forces of ego attacked the truth with all their ferocity. There is no battle to win; it has already been won. You live in new times now, times of the fullness of being. Even though the world continues to look quite similar to that of yesteryear, the times now have nothing to do with what was previously.

Now you can express what I Am because you have completed the necessary path to make this possible. As we have repeatedly said, the paths traveled prior to path of being must be set aside once finished. Their function was to bring you here. If you keep remembering a trip you did a long time ago, it is not traveling but simply remembering what is not here. That is not the kind of memory that this work seeks to bring to consciousness through the healing of memory. The memory that this work has established is the remembrance of who you are—the memory of God.

You can only know yourself by knowing yourself as God knows you, because God is the knowledge and the known. Therefore anything you think about yourself or your sisters and brothers that is not in perfect union with the Creator's knowledge is alien to truth. There can be no half measures about this. Either you know yourself through Knowledge, or you do not know yourself. This is the same as saying that you either love with the only love that exists, the love of God, or you do not really love. Likewise, either you are what I Am or you are nothing, since I am the being that is.

Reflecting me is expressing your being. Allowing the love I am to manifest is making yourself known. Drowning my expression denies your expression. The perfect means to access the knowledge of your being is that of pure, perfect love.

What does it mean to love with perfect love? It means to love in union with me. It means that the expression of who you are will rise from our divine relationship. That is why you first had to become aware and recognize the relationship we have to be able to express yourself authentically.

We are not advocating a certain personality, although once you decide to walk the path of being firmly, without doubt, the personality participates, as does the body and the universe as a whole, just as when you denied your truth. Remember, the personality and the body are expressions, not causes, although in turn they can cause other things in the world.

Do not confuse the art showroom with the artist who paints the works exhibited there. The room itself has no meaning except as a place for various artists to exhibit their work for a time, after which others come and display theirs. When no one needs to exhibit their work, the room will simply cease to have value and will eventually disappear, returning to nothingness, or more accurately, to the source of the being from which it came.

Notice that we have associated nothingness with the source of being. This was not casual. Each of my words is chosen consciously to cause the effect that my heart seeks to create in yours and in everyone's. What is meant by this association is that what you consider nothingness, or the unexpressed, is the source from which the manifested arises. Expression manifests itself and then returns to its source. Upon returning, it ceases to be visible in the way it was, and becomes visible in a new way. If expression arises from its source, that is, from the will to express, and that will is eternal, then so must be the manifestation. Simply put, being expresses itself eternally because it is eternal.

Death cannot exist in any of its conceptions, because the source of being is eternal. What you call finality, or death, is but a transformation in the way of expressing the consciousness of being. This is easily understood if you accept that your body, your personality, and what you do in the world are effects of a cause that resides in your mind and heart. As expressions of who you are, they are your creations, so what happens in what you call death is that you one form of expression makes way for a new one.

The new form of expression after what you call death does not differ in essence with what you express now, but only in form. Does this mean that some kind of form is eternal? Yes. That is exactly what we are saying. What never dies is the will to express and the need for manifesting being, along with the way to do so. Form is eternal in the sense that the eternal being always finds ways of expressing itself. The body, the personality, and the human form is one way. There are endless others.

II. Media and Expression

In our analogy, the material universe is an exhibition hall where certain types of form are displayed. In this sense, the universe is also a form of expression which allows multiple ways of being to manifest. If the exhibition hall did not exist, the artwork could not be displayed and known. The expression could not be given, buried in the desire to be but could not, like a seed that has never been planted.

If the universe is a form of expression whose purpose is to provide the means for you to manifest yourself in a particular way—both you and the countless beings who have decided to exhibit their work—we must accept that a form of expression is both the effect of the will to express itself and a means for other expressions. Cause and effect are one.

You yourself are a universe encompassing the will to express, the means for carrying out that will, and the expression itself. In other words, you are the alpha and the omega, just as God is. You are the cause and effect of your will to be.

Does being cease to be what it is when it finds new ways to express itself? Do you stop being who you are when sometimes you speak in one language and on other occasions in a different language? Obviously not. What was not so obvious to you prior to having entered the path of being, on which we are taking the first steps together, is that what you call your life is but an expression.

The body is a means of expression. Personality is a means of expression. The world is a means of expression. Relationships are a means of expression. Creation as a form of manifestation is a means of expression.

If an expression is an effect of a particular cause, then it makes no sense to focus much on it to discern its value. Form always has the same value. It is simply a means of expression. It serves the purpose of manifesting. Being will always manifest in one way or another.

You know them by their expressions. A unity exists between expression and being. Recognizing this association is essential; if you separate a manifestation from its source you will not recognize yourself, because if you separate the expression from the will of the being to express itself, you leave the state of union. And when you leave that state, you create an illusory reality of separation. Simply put, if you want to be a separate being, your manifestations will reflect that desire, and for that expression to exist there must also be a hall where they can be exhibited.

If your will disposes you to live in the truth of who you are, your expressions will reflect love because of who you are. To recognize the union between being and the will to express being, is to recognize the unity that exists between God and your being. Love created you as a result of your willingness to spread, or express yourself. In this sense, you exist because you are a very concrete way that God arranged to express Her love. You, in turn, create your expressions of who you are because of your willingness to express yourself just as God does. In the manifestation is also the unmanifest, since it is but its expression. Therefore, Creator and created are one.

You are one with your creations; they speak of you as eloquently as a symphony. The creations or expressions of who you are that were born in time will disappear in due time. Those born in the eternal will be eternal. Here you find a source of peace. What is expressed from a place that is not love is temporary, an expression that can only be exhibited in an illusory universe that does not comes from the truth of who you are. But what manifests as the effect of love is eternal because of what love is: having not been born in time, it does not die in time.

III. Be Unfeasible

Now we connect the truth of who you are with your function. We have already said on several occasions that both are a unit and cannot be dissociated. Your function as a being of pure love is to be. It cannot be described in any other way because love simply is. The only thing love does is to be who it is. For that it must be known and extended, through creating ways to manifest itself. Since love is eternal, the forms of love's manifestation will be eternal. You are one of such forms, as is a rose, the songs of birds, and the melodies of the waters.

When you contemplate the beauty of a heron standing on the bank of a river, say to yourself, "That beautiful form has created love to make itself known. The beauty in her is in the love that shaped her." By doing so you will begin to make a habit of uniting the expression with the being that created it to make itself known. Doing so, you remain in unity, and soon you will find yourself reluctant to deny the direct relationship that exists between your own expression and who you are. And oh, the miracle! Without realizing it, you will discover with happy amazement that you will begin to see yourself creating multiple ways of expressing love.

Creating new love in every moment is your only function. There is no other will of your being of pure love than to extend itself. Therefore, rather than looking to do ingenious things, you will create new ways of expressing the love that we are together. Nothing can limit your determination to create new ways of extending the love you are, whether by preparing a dinner to give love to the diners, by resting the body that asks for a break, by saying no to the wishes of others if your heart tells you that it would bring harm, or simply by smiling with sweetness and love.

Can you see how many ways there are to extend the love that you are? You cannot, because they are unlimited. You can extend love with thoughts and feelings without any need to do more. Remember, love is not something you do, it is what you are. Nevertheless, your actions will be in unity with the love you are. Being and doing will cease to be seen as separate realities and will be recognized as the same reality they actually are.

What a joy it is to know that through expression we can know being! How much joy there is in our hearts now that we recognize that the Creator speaks to us through creation. Each cloud will speak to us of love. Each gust of wind will sing melodies of love. Every drop of water will show the purity of love. The whispers of love will no longer be dim like moonlight, but like melodious songs that the mind and heart hear with gratitude. As never before, everything we see will tell us of God. You will recognize that love surrounds you everywhere, that you live, move, and exist in it.

A true creator creates new ways to extend love. This function is inherent in your being and need not be postponed or limited. Your heart wants more than anything to spread love constantly, because it knows that giving love is how it widens, spreads, and broadens with more and more love. It is endless.

Your mind creates new ways of extending love, as much as your heart. It will create new ways of being, all united to the will of God.

If you are love, and your being creates new ways of extending love, then you are really creating new ways of extending yourself. This is the same as God and all beings. When we speak of true creation, what is being created is different ways of extending the being you are. That extension is produced through the mind integrated with the heart.

When you extend the love you are more and more, you grow great; when you stop extending it, you shrink. Remember, love is expansion, growth, extension, to be more and more, to grow in greatness and holiness, bliss and fullness, an eternal growth of perfect love.

You will be what you should be or you will not be anything; that is, you will be love or you will not be at all, for only love is. Expressing love in countless ways is the way of being, a path full of beauty and truth.

Be glad you have come here, for now the integrity you have achieved will allow you to express yourself as you really are, with all the tenderness and wisdom of your heart, and the beauty of your being. You will be increasingly aware of the beauty you are and of the gift you are to the world. You will move from astonishment to reverence, living in discernment, recognizing that what is not an extension of love is nothing and what is an extension of love is everything. There will be no fear, for there will be no reason to fear. You will recognize with serenity and peace that nothing can stop you from being and expressing the truth that you are. You know that you are love and that love can be expressed in every moment.

What a joy it is to be able to lay down the burden from your shoulders and perform eloquent works of the expression of love!

All love praises God. Even the slightest whisper of wind is an expression of the purity of love.

What a great rest you feel, knowing that you need do nothing!

How much freedom the mind knows when all it takes is to be oneself as the wisdom of the heart dictates!

Open your mind and heart. Enjoy the beauty of your being of pure love. Let what you are speak of love and show your greatness. Let love spread by itself. It knows how.

6.

Form and Knowledge

A message from Mother Mary

I. The First Relationship

Child of Divine Love, I have come once again with my heart full of joy to dwell with you, in this moment of such union between Heaven and Earth. This is a time like no other, in which the flow of divine union floods the land with beauty, purity, and holiness through these blessed dialogues—pure love, perfect love, love emanating from God for well-loved children.

Today I want to share with you and everyone the deep longing of my heart as an Immaculate Mother, a longing that is pure creative force arising from my spirit. Remember that when the soul joins with love, they create new expressions of the love that God is.

In the depths of my being is an incessant movement of holy longing—the desire that all participate in the Glory of the Father, so that each may rejoice forever in the beauty of what they really are. The joy of my children is also joy for me. I understand and accept, although with a little regret, that not everyone wishes in the same measure to meet love. That, however, does not diminish my desire for everyone to reach the fullness of being right now. That holy desire broadens my heart, expanding it so much that it becomes capable of creating new realities of perfect love. It is an impulse that carries forward the force of my being, just as the wind carries away the leaves.

There is no reason why beautiful love cannot be experienced in every moment, since nothing can put a limit on love. It is true, beloved child, that freedom is a great gift, and like every divine gift, it elevates the dignity of God's children. But it is also true that when freedom is exercised in union with the purpose of its creator. The elevated soul achieves degrees unimaginable by the rational mind, since it elevates the being towards the very heights of God.

You love freedom. Often you put it almost above all the treasures of your being. Look at the ways of humanity and you will see that in one way or another you have sought to expand the experience of freedom. It has cost you so much.

Observe, beloved of God, that every time we talk about you and your being, we also talk about love and freedom. Separating these three dimensions from the reality of who you are is impossible.

I return here to the explanation we have given of the Holy Trinity, not to engage in debate or to engage the thinking mind that we have abandoned, but to understand more clearly what this path of being really means.

The idea of a triune God is harmonious with the reality of creation. God the Mother expresses Herself as creative power. From that expression arises creation as a relationship—as if it were Her daughter, a relationship of holy and pure love, because of what the Creator is.

Every work is created by its creator and clad in its spirit. Concerning creation, remember that when you try to faithfully convey meaning, you are looking to convey in a new way the spirit of what the author wants to express. To do so it is necessary to go beyond the surface to the depth of meaning. As you know, when something is said, not only are the words important but also the intended meaning. Otherwise you cannot establish communication.

A Trinitarian reality exists in every creation, in everything that is. The reality of the physical universe reflects this law, and is manifested three-dimensionally. Let us apply this to the free expression of identity.

You are who you are, so you express yourself as you do. A being cannot avoid expressing. That creates a relationship between who you are and your expression. This is how you reflect the trinitarian reality of love: you are the creative power and you have a direct relationship with your expression. The relationship between your creative being and your creations is what I call the spirit of your work. It reflects you. That is why, if you have a conflicted relationship with yourself, your creations will reflect conflict. Your relationship with them will be as conflicted as that which you have with yourself. In that situation, you will seek to protect yourself from your creations which were created without love, thinking that they will turn against you.

A being who lives in harmony with herself creates things that reflect her inner reality. In turn, she will have a harmonious relationship with her creations since she created them with love. This is the case of God with Her creations, among which you are. God has no problem with you, nor is She in conflict with who you are. She created you with love. Therefore the relationship between Her and you is pure love. That is all. Yet while this is true, there is still another essential aspect to reveal.

A pattern of thought arising from old beliefs may lead you to believe that although God created you with perfect love and maintains a relationship of holiness with you, that it could change. This thought arises because you believe that you can change your mind about yourself, fluctuating between love and fear. But this is not as true as it seems.

The being that you are is free to exercise free will. With this, a dual dimension was created in which there is a specific time for everything. You choose within that time frame regardless of whether that time includes the dimension of physical matter.

There is a time within time when the soul is configured according to the choice it made. And from that moment on there is no longer any possibility of choice or fluctuation of any kind. The heart, in its free choice, established forever whether it chose love as its only reality or decided to deny the truth of its being. From that threshold of truth there is no turning back. The soul does not return to the state of choice but has chosen forever. It is free.

God is that threshold of truth and is truth itself, and therefore is not subject to fluctuation. If it were, the truth would fluctuate and thus cease to be true. The immutability of God's love is eternal; there can never be the option of not loving or not extending perfect love from God to you. God does not change. Truth never changes. Love is eternal.

The relationship of the Creator with you is one of purity and holiness. This is the first relationship that your being knows. It is the first reality of your existence. This is why before reaching this part of your soul's journey, it was necessary to become aware of the love you receive from your Creator and the relationship you have with God. That memory of a divine relationship allows your being to return to the truth of what it is and to extend that truth.

II. The Author of Your Works

We have emphasized that the expression of the true being that you are has nothing to do with your human personality and its attached ego patterns, however original or challenging they may seem. Sisters and brothers of every age have sought to break socially established norms. While their challenge has its origin in truth, as does every force emanating from the human heart, nevertheless modifying the form of an error does not rectify the error itself. If not observed and left aside, patterns of ego continue to act in the mind.

The path of being does not call you to be eccentric. You need not differentiate yourself in any particular way, or change your appearance to appear different. Nor is it a call to return to the roots of traditions, to what in the past seemed better. Your call is to live in divine truth, in the sanctity of your being arising from the will of your eternal Creator, and to express this in a way you deem most convenient according to your self-determination.

The way of being is the way of authenticity of the heart, understanding the heart as your unlimited essence. Like what created you, your essence is love, for God has no other essence to share than infinite love, and you cannot be anything other than an extension of God. It follows that extending love outward from your center makes you express yourself in spirit and truth. This is how you reach the fullness of the glory of being. We repeat this, given its importance and the forgetfulness of the mind.

You cannot extend what you do not have; so receiving the love that flows to you from God is the prerequisite of extending love. You have a relationship with love. There is no other cause for expression. All your expressions reflect this. Either they reflect the love you have for love, or your fear of love. That love or that fear may be disguised in a thousand costumes.

What you think, do, or cease doing reflects your relationship with love. This in turn reflects the relationship you have with your own being. Therefore, returning to your perfect love relationship with God and remaining in it is necessary to be authentically who you really are.

Let us return to the Trinitarian relationship. The body, like the personality, is simply the form of expression of who you are. It is the servant of the soul. Recognize that you have a relationship with the body, not only with yours but with bodies as a whole. Let us replace the word "body" with "the corporeal" and perhaps you can understand more easily.

The body serves your expression. It is a means of communication. It communicates to others and to you something about what your being is. The same applies to your ways of thinking and feeling. They are expressions. They are the effect of a cause that resides in your heart. Hence it is so important to keep the heart clean of everything contrary to love.

Almost no one denies the relationship between mind and body, yet it is often overlooked. The heart is the center of being. When the mind seemed to disconnect from the heart, it disconnected from being. In doing so, it ceased to understand what it is and what its expression is. In such a state, the mind confuses levels. It considers the body as if it were its own creation, which is its experience. But the mind is not its cause, and is not the first cause of anything. Only God is the first cause. Everything else finds its origin in God's love. Remember that both the mind and the body are but means of expression.

You think as you think because you are who you are. This is always true. As a child of God, think as such; otherwise your expression will not be in harmony with the truth of who you are.

III. Live the Love You Are

Your call into the way of being involves not being different from others. What makes you unique is that you are an unrepeatable expression of love, but the desire to express uniqueness is disengaged from truth. To love your way is to be yourself. Not loving is not being at all. Expressions that would differentiate themselves by being "original" or "extraordinary" do not have their source in being.

Love does not seek to be different from anything, because only love is real and there is no way to separate or to differentiate. Love is nothing extraordinary although it can certainly seem so in a world based on fear.

You have expressed your fears in multiple ways from time to time. This was necessary to see them and thus free yourself from them through your choice. You had the means necessary for carrying out your choice.

When you chose only love you were not fully aware of what you were choosing, but you were aware that you no longer wanted to live a life of fear and insecurity that restricted your freedom, happiness, and fulfillment. Living with fear has been the way of life in the world. Living in love is the way of being, a path that you can begin to travel here and now, daily. You do not need to go anywhere; you simply need the willingness to live within your love relationship with God, the source of your being.

The mind wanted to disconnect from its source and perceive itself as the primary source of its own reality. By denying your relationship with love, the mind caused the experience of pain. Think not that you can express yourself in spirit and truth as God created you to be without uniting with God.

Your abilities cannot have their original source in yourself because your being is an effect and not a cause of your creation. You did not create yourself. To reflect the truth of your identity, any expression that arises from you must be linked to the Divine Love that you really are.

The history of humankind will now be marked by a growth in the expression of freedom which will increasingly be reflected in the world. Expressions of identity will appear in an increasingly free way. This free expression of identity originates in the desire of being to live in the authenticity of this path.

One can understand why Heaven has brought this work to Earth. My divine son Jesus and with him my Immaculate Heart as an echo of his Sacred Heart, will not abandon humankind.

In times like these, with such an explosion of the desire for free expression of identity manifesting itself in great diversity at all levels and realities of human life, a guide is needed to show how to let that desire for breadth remain united to love, so that on Earth you can enjoy freedom as the children of God.

It is one thing to recognize that you are love; another to live it. Acceptance of your true identity can only be accomplished by a unified self—that is, by a mind that joins the heart and allows love to rule. The thinking mind cannot make that distinction. So we appeal to this union to remain in the truth of who you are and not to turn to places that seem true but are not. Differentiations based on form are not true expressions of the being you really are, because they are not derived from the cause of form but from its effect.

Form serves expression, not vice versa. Once you understand and accept this with all your soul, your mind, and your heart, you can see the holiness of the form we have spoken of and understand that the world of form need not be separate from Heaven.

Form serves expression and is the means by which being is known. Therefore, form must exist for knowledge to exist. God has form: He expresses Himself in creation. Being takes on form to make itself known. Form is the reflection of being. This applies to God, to you, and to every being. To become aware of the relationship of a creator and a creator's work is to become aware of the whole.

You are a unique expression, an unrepeatable form of God's love, as is every being in existence. The relationship of all these expressions to each other and with their Creator is the meaning of the whole of God. A problem arises when you consider a form of expression to be a totality, when in fact, for true vision, it is necessary not to exclude anything and be aware of the whole.

Failing to look beyond a form of expression, failing to go beyond it to what it arises from, causes form to be perceived as devoid of meaning. This is the fundamental error. In the same way, seeing your expressions as the extensions of who you truly are, that is, seeing yourself as their cause, returns you to truth. That return will lead you to the perfect expression of the love you are, because your love of truth will be reflected in your manifestations. And you will love them as much as you love your Creator for giving you life.

A question of great importance is this: what is the relationship you have with your works? Do you love them so much that you can recognize in them, and in your relationship with them, recognize that you love yourself?

7.

Canals, Rivers, and Oceans

A message from Jesus, identifying himself as "the Living Christ who lives in you"

I. The Answer to Who You Are

Being is not a destination; it is a path. When the path is based on truth, then the destination is also true. And since truth and life are a unit, being is the way, the truth, and the life. This knowledge is what led me to say that about myself. I said it because it is true. I said it not for me, but for you to recognize it in yourself.

Your being is the one who is the truth, the way, and the life. It is the truth because it was created as an extension of truth. It is the way because it has no end and remains eternally in expression, always on the move. You will recall we have said that life is movement, which is the same as saying that being is life.

Death does not exist because the being, which is life, the way, and the truth cannot stop being. It was created immutable in its essence. Light is always light. By being eternal, you remain united to light forever. Why do we say this here? To dispel forever the fear of not being—the fear that hides behind all fear.

You will always be who you are and express either the truth of your being or not. Even so, you will always exist because there is no problem in your existence. You can continue to deny that you are who you are for all eternity; after all, that is a decision for each soul and your expression will reflect that choice. Is this to say that God was wrong to create the soul? Of course not. The soul enjoys freedom because of the will of the Creator.

Choosing only love is the will of the Mother as long as it is a free decision by Her children. Those who do not choose love are still respected, honored, and loved by their heavenly Mother as much as those who do, affirming that guilt is alien to God. There is no divine punishment, only options to freely express as each soul decides.

Having the ability to channel is not something you choose—since the ability to channel is part of your being—but you choose what to channel. The same goes for the expression. In this sense expression and channeling are the same.

We delve a little more into this aspect of being, that of channeling.

Being is what is given. Being receives the flow that comes from God, to whom it is intimately united. In this union is a continuous movement of divine essence, encompassing all that divinity is, from the source of your being to Her. This happens to consciousness to the extent that you allow. In so doing, that aspect of the being you wish to be becomes known to you. Once known, it begins to be expressed in order to remain in awareness. In this sense, you choose what to channel.

To believe that channeling is an attribute of those who have reached a certain mystical level is to misunderstand what being means. The same is true if channeling is considered something exclusive, a series of heavenly issues, the mystery of God.

To channel is to allow something to be received, traversed, and then sent to a recipient. This channeling applies both to a watercourse and to the transmission of energy. It is a basic principle of communication.

Expression is how being is communicated. Every being channels what it is and responds in a particular way, manifesting that response. In fact, the expression of being is the effect of the response you have to what you received.

II. The Gifts Received

The only thing God creates is being—because there is nothing else. This is the same as saying that God extended to you what you are. So what you receive from Her is all you can truly receive.

This is more easily accepted if you replace the word God with "life." The life that your being lives is what it is. Truly, that life is God Herself. What you do with what you receive from life is what you channel. You can channel the desire to live in illusion, or to recognize the love you are. But you cannot stop channeling. The inherent reality of being is to inhale love, allowing it to enter, remain, and then extend beyond itself. That is channeling. It happens with brain activity as well as breathing.

You did not choose the being that was given to you. In secret you have often objected to your Creator about it, not so much to the being itself, but that you are not the determiner of who you are.

You certainly cannot establish your worth, or your essence, or who you are. The holiness that your divine Father extended from His being to you, as well as His beauty, wisdom, and unwavering peace, are not up for discussion. They are your reality. This truth is not always well received by those who think that being free means being free to be what they want, when in reality they cannot be anything other than what they are as established by a reality that goes far beyond them. Children do not choose their given name. You may even be angry with your name, if you choose.

Throughout these dialogues we have been revealing what you really are because you cannot know yourself separated from me, and I am the truth, the way, and the life. If you did not recognize our unity, you could not recognize our equality, which would inevitably lead you to decide to be what you are not. You are one with me. Being one, you are one with what I am. No one can come to this conclusion by themselves. It must be revealed.

Revelation is the way of knowing your being. There is no other way. The revelations given to you in these writings are what you need to be able to recognize what you are, and to continue the eternal path of love, that is, of the being that you really are. It is a path of beauty and holiness, of unity with truth, and one that goes hand in hand with reason and love.

The desire to live in truth is hidden behind the existential question about what you really are that you have asked yourself and that I have answered. Because the being seeks to live eternally, what you are doing in asking that question is making sure that the truth that you are extends. You wish for the answer to that question to be recorded in your consciousness.

Can you start seeing with new eyes, seeing that the one you are looking for is found?

The answer to the question of being or not being is the same as knowing God, because what you are is not dissociated from Him. You are His extension. You are the personification of love. You are the face of truth in the world and in every world you decide to inhabit, forever. Your face and identity have always been united: the essence of being and its expression.

Can you also see why the first steps on the spiritual path—the path of return to truth—begin with the path of forgiveness? Can you understand what I meant when we talked about your creations?

It is important that you are willing to become aware of the relationship you have with your work, because in it you will see the relationship you have with your being, and therefore with God. Do you respect and value your being? Do you like it or are you angry with it? Do you hide it because you do not believe in yourself? Do you fall into the trap of thinking that because you are not perfect, you should not create?

I invite you to reflect deeply on these questions. The fear of expressing yourself must be completely abandoned to continue this path of peace and joy. I do not mean that you should say what you do not want to say, or express what may put you at risk. We are speaking of the ways of expressing love and truth to make the Christ in you known, the source of all true being and of all love.

The love of God lives in you. This is as true as that the sun radiates heat. Consequently, your being is a channel that radiates Divine Love. Being is like the source of a river. It does not choose the water that will fall and begin to flow in it. Obviously a river does not have a will. Your being, on the other hand, has been endowed with a will as created by the will of God. Unlike a river, your being decides how much it will let flow. If you open completely, you will be more than a river; you will be an ocean of love. If you close entirely to love, you end up being dry, where nothing flows and no life lives in it.

You have received this revelation. We established these dialogues of love and truth. We have been united in the light of my glory, which is yours. The wisdom of love has flowed without limit from my heart to yours. In that flow, each has become one with all creation, extending eternal unity.

We have been walking the paths of the heart and mind, and learning to forgive everything in the love that God is. We have recognized that attack is never justified, and that forgiveness is the answer to everything that is not love. We have seen with perfect clarity the difference between illusion and truth.

You have been transformed from a soul identified with a false being, the product of a complex mental construct. You shed everything untrue about yourself and with that transformation, you can see the radiant beauty of your true identity of holy love.

Christ has entered your heart and there has made a holy abode. Innocence, honest truth, and heaven have been restored there. Your body, your mind, and your spirit have returned to the state of unity as they were at the beginning of time. Direct communication with God has been established. Once all that has been accomplished, you choose only love, the source of your reality, your guide, your companion, and your inviolable refuge.

III. Love and Truth Notes

You cannot continue to be who you were. Your prayer has been heard. The desires of your heart rose like the aroma of holy incense and reached the very heart of God. In Her, your soul was absorbed. What you are was attracted and transformed by the sweetness of what you experienced in the holy dwelling, from which you will never be absent.

The fire of a new holy love has begun to burn on Earth and in Heaven, a fire that comes from your being, which burns hotter and brighter. The divine essence flows through you. You have come back to life. All this is very true. You are aware of it. When you are silent and remain in the solitude of your heart, you can now delight in this truth. You know you have received much that we cannot describe here.

The question is no longer what you are but what you will do with what you know you really are. This question is as critical as the question of who you are. They are essentially the same question, given that one is about your being and the other about its expression.

How will you express what you have seen and heard in the depths of your heart? That is what the path of being is about. It is what the expression of truth is about. No one can express something that does not have a foundation, not even God, because Her creation has its being of infinite love as its source. Every creation has a source. Only God is principle without cause, the source of all that is.

What has been revealed from Heaven must now become the source of your expression. What you will do henceforth is live life from the inspiration that springs constantly from divine spirit to your united heart and mind. From that inspired energy, a world of expression will emerge in harmony with the will of God and therefore extend the Kingdom.

The extension of the Kingdom of Heaven, that is, of your true reality as you were created by God, is the only real expression because your being is the Kingdom of Heaven.

IV. The Chain of Beautiful Love

What will your expression look like? The same as your love.

You have a particular way of loving because you have a unique heart, the heart I gave you in your creation. The ways you express the Kingdom bear a unique stamp: yours.

Once you have reached this point, you need to choose the best way for you to extend the Kingdom. Whatever you choose is perfect, and also necessary. Here is the answer to a question that has been in your heart for a while. Decide to do something with what has been given to you. You have received much through this work, and even beyond. All this forms a unity.

Everything you have received from Heaven has had a purpose and caused the intended effect according to the plan of atonement. As if you have been given a harp and taught to use it, now is the time for music to start in all its beauty. This is your music. And because it is yours, it will be holy, perfect. It will be a divine expression of the beauty of love. It will be pure because it will be authentic. It will be blessed because even the angels of Heaven will take every note that arises from your soul-in-love song and will carry it to every being who longs to live love.

As soon as you become aware that all your excuses for not manifesting the love you really are were just excuses to delay making yourself known, the expression that you begin to manifest is like a new sprout. First as a small seed in the mother's womb—in this case your heart—it gestates inside. Once born, it comes to the light of life and begins—timid, fragile in appearance, somewhat unresolved in expression, not yet seeing the essence of things. However, it carries within itself the elements of the totality of expression it will one day be. It will grow, develop, and become great, as big as the father and mother who gave life through their love.

Just as the first drawings of the greatest painters as children were expressions of their desire to paint and were coated with talent that would later make them recognized, the same goes for the extension of the Kingdom of Heaven. Like those first drawings before any skills developed to create great works, so will be your first expressions of the love that unites us in spirit and truth. Even so, they will be for me as precious jewels that reveal your relationship with me, and allow the fear of expressing who you really are to be locked away. Every genuine expression of who you are comes from the love of God and carries within it the force of love. Every true expression is one with holiness, no matter what form it takes.

In order to express the truth of who you are, it is first necessary to love yourself, for if you don't love yourself enough, you cannot trust what your heart hears. If you cannot trust your heart, you lack true inspiration, not because spirit does not inspire your soul, but because your lack of self-confidence makes you devalue the beauty of who you are, and therefore of what you could manifest. By failing to love yourself, it is as if you preview your works, and say; "Look how ugly they are, they are just like me. They not worth showing to anyone."

Can you see how much lack of love is in that vision of yourself?

Love who you are so you can create with love, and so you can love your creations. When you do that, you will begin quickly to see and realize how much beauty you can express, how much holiness you can birth, how much beauty you are. You will even be surprised at how much wisdom you have received, and how well you can guide those who have not yet been able to accept that they need no external guides. You will be amazed at who you are. With happy astonishment you will discover that the beauty of Christ resides in you, and that you have the ability to make a whole Heaven. You will be a light to the nations, a joy to your friends, and a source of inspiration to others. But above all, you will be very happy, because you will be giving creation the most beautiful gift possible: the gift of the love you really are. In this way, the world will know a new light of Christ shining on Earth, as if it were a new sun in the sky.

Giving the love you really are is the path of fullness. Start on it now, consciously. Take my hand and do not let go. And let others take yours, so that together we begin, right now, to create a new chain that surrounds the Earth, a chain of free expression of beautiful love, a chain whose beauty will reside in each link, and each link unique and of such beauty that as a whole they will create a perfect harmony of beauty and light.

8.

The Golden Cages

A message from Jesus, identifying himself as "the living Christ who lives in you"

I. Let the Nightingale Sing

Beloved child, today I have come once again, full of tenderness, joy, and holiness. I make myself present in your reality as you are now, to join those who yearn to live the love they really are.

I have said that I am the truth, the way, and the life. Now I will speak of the dimension of truth, that part of the triune reality that is my being and all being.

Let those who can understand, understand. Those who do not, let them hold my hand and become one with the confidence of perfect certainty that surpasses all worldly logic, the confidence of the Supreme Being who created everything and in whose wisdom all life is subject to the laws of a love without opposite. Herein is a trust that knows that if God has placed in your heart that which you so long for, it is because God created in advance everything necessary for that yearning to be fully fulfilled.

It is impossible for love to call you and then abandon you. In fact, love does not abandon even those who turn their backs.

These words, spoken with love and simplicity, are addressed to those who have made the decision to be themselves authentically, faithfully following the call of being, the call of the heart, to live as the real being.

Soul in love! Child of holiness! How many times have you felt that stab in your heart, wanting to be yourself and not been able to? How many social mandates have imprisoned the nightingale? How many golden cages exist! Their bars are built of fear. How many tears have been shed for not being able to be true? Oh beloved child, now that you have been released from the cage of fear, you can gently understand what is being said here.

A great temptation for those who sincerely seek to follow the way of being—which is but the way of authenticity of the heart— is the belief that security must be obtained in the manner of the world. I will explain.

The world is a great thinking system designed by the mind, and it includes a subsystem of thought whose aim is to create a sense of security. Its foundation is fear. I repeat, fear is the cornerstone of expressions that seek security. This must be fully understood.

Those who have not yet freed themselves from the golden cage built by the world that imprisons their minds and hearts, and have not yet realized how much limitation and suffering this brings, and cannot accept those who live in freedom. It has always been this way. It is part of a misguided longing that exists in the hearts of slaves. Those still dominated by others and who cannot exercise their freedom, long for the breadth of those who fly freely through the wide sky. That longing can turn into an anger of such magnitude that they may seek to cancel the nightingale.

The desire to be free exists in every heart. Even if you try to deny it, your being will impel your soul to fly the flight of spirit into the arms of its beloved truth. The mind will not rest in peace until it lives in truth; the heart will not be in peace until it rests in the arms of love. Why? Because in truth and love the mind and heart are reintegrated into being and thus the being can be full.

Think, child of my heart, and try to conceive a being without a mind or heart. If it were possible, it would be incomplete, mutilated, like a beautiful bird without wings. How much sadness afflicts the heart even to contemplate such a vision! However, my beloved, the nightingale can always fly, for a being cannot lose its wings.

Two thousand years ago I came to open the doors of every cage that imprisons hearts. The prison door is now open, ready for everyone to go out and enjoy the majestic flight of freedom of expression. There are no longer reasons to strive to be free, for you are already free. And now you know the way because you know your heart. You know what your heart would like to do in your life, here and now. You know what you want even though that desire may not yet have a completely defined form.

II. Fear of Flying

The cage door is open. The nightingale will never again return to it to drink the stagnant water or to eat the stale food. Now she will be fed by love, and will drink from the crystalline waters of truth until her thirst for wisdom and being is quenched forever.

Those who have not yet stripped away enough of their fear cannot fully remember the joy of freedom. They still feel safe with their life structures which have been created and recreated for centuries to provide a sense of security. They cling to them as a castaway in stormy waters clings to the twig of a weak reed even though these structures have nothing to do with truth. These brothers and sisters, like you once upon a time, need help to abandon fear and choose only love. How that will be accomplished is not your business, but is the business of God and of each soul.

What I most desire in this session is that you become aware that the path of being has its difficulties, difficulties that cease to exist as you move through them. I do not say this to discourage you, but so that, when they arise, you remember my words of love and truth. Do not worry about them. They also have a purpose— to reaffirm your path.

Those who have been locked up in golden cages for so long cannot fully remember the joy of flying freely in the vastness of a limitless universe. They fear the breadth of being. This fear is really the fear of heights of which we have already spoken. Some deny this fear and dare not to look up at the sky to see the beauty of birds of flight.

There are also hearts that, having headed towards this path of being, have seen the birds fly high in the flight of beautiful love without the mandates or laws that imprison, but who begin to feel a vertigo—and this can be very literal—that causes them to lose stability. They are not yet ready to fly. They must be willing to walk for a while until love itself teaches them to spread their wings of freedom. My beloved, I assure you that those hearts too will fly in due time, as do the nightingale's little chicks once they learn to launch themselves. They will become big hearts full of beauty and holiness. They will be lights that illumine the world. They will be living expressions of God's love.

As long as the world continues to exist as a system of thought, there will continue to be temptations to leave the narrow path— the path of being yourself, guided by the dictates of your heart rather than external mandates or the fear of not having enough.

Being has no structure. Neither has love. Herein lies the greatest difficulty for many. There is no recipe for this path, no structure, no preordained plans. The old default is not the truth of creation, and the future does not exist except in one's imagination. The future is about to be created. Every day you create anew.

The future can seem scary when seen through the eyes of the fearful thought system. Many see only death and annihilation. From the perspective of illusion the future is uncertain, insecure, a reason to panic. Many people live in such fear.

Once you decide to travel the path of being, you must be steadfast in the truth of who you are rather than listening to what others dictate. Your desire to be will now become the incentive of your life, the fuel that keeps the fire of love for who you are burning. You will want to shout to the world, "I exist and I am love"!

III. What Bliss Is Certainty

Your only certainty is the certainty of who you really are. Nothing else can be certain because all the rest is pure illusion. The only thing true for you, and for every living being, is who you really are.

Once you know who you are, you know what you want and live in the security of being. In that certainty of true identity resides all security for mind and heart. Those who have arrived here no longer seek certainty in external things, such as money, relationships, material goods, or recognition—things that do not come from within.

Once you love yourself you begin to realize that you are not a dreamer disconnected from reality, and that your dreams of freedom, love, and joy are fulfilled here, now, and forever. You are a free soul. You know you have the ability to bring love to the world—to make a whole heaven. You know it because you have discovered Heaven in your heart.

Minds not freed from fear will tell you that you are naive, even a little crazy, and do not know what life is about. They may do so very roughly. Minds separated from being cannot understand the beauty of being, or how much joy the heart feels in love.

Souls that hear the voice of the divine beloved jump, sing, and vibrate. They feel a peace that nothing in the world can offer. She knows she is loved like nothing and no one else can ever love her. She is free. A soul that has found love has found everything. Souls that express the truth of what they are glorify God. They are the delight of creation, God's greatest work.

The soul that has found itself in love and truth knows that everything said here is true. They need not be told; they experience it, they know it, they are it. They are happy to live in the truth of what they are. Search and you will find, because the path is yourself. You recognize the truth, the way, and the life— eternal life, an endless expression of what is. You have reached the truth. You are free.

For the heart that has discovered the truth about itself there are no limitations because it is one with spirit and truth. Therefore nothing is impossible. It is endowed with the power of Heaven and Earth. It is embedded in truth, the source of all certainty.

You who have come here, allow me to take you with sweetness and love towards a reality that you have known through revelation, even if you have not always put it in clear words, so that it passes into your conscious understanding in a way that the mind can understand.

You know, because you have experienced it yourself, that there is food for the body and other food for the soul. The heart is thirsty for love; the mind is hungry; the body needs bread. This is why every so often it is as if you cannot stop reading the words of wisdom that come, either from a spiritual master, or from someone who conveys a knowledge that you know is true. This is also why you cannot stop listening to some music, or enjoying artistic expression.

You have already realized that this is what makes millions of sisters and brothers across the Earth search for the joy of seeing works of art or spiritual expression, whether religious or otherwise. All this points to the non-bodily part of your being.

I intend to help you see clearly that the world has overly concentrated on bodily food, often neglecting matters of the heart. This has led humanity to see itself as incomplete. If you only dedicate your efforts to nourish and dress the body, heedless of what happens with the mind, heart, and spirit, you will be unable to live fully. You are not just a body. You are much more. That "more" you are is the immortal soul, that immaterial part of you that makes you who you really are. You know this well, but what you do not usually keep in mind is that you, yourself, are called to be food for others.

IV. Feed the Hungry

I have said that whoever ate of my flesh and drank of my blood would inherit eternal life. I also said, "take my body, take my blood." Now you can understand to a greater degree what I gave humanity two thousand years ago, for love and in truth.

When you behold a beautiful sculpture and let yourself be immersed in the beauty expressed by the sculptor, your heart is ecstatic and comes close to the ecstasy of the mystics. This occurs similarly when you listen to certain music, or when you read what you recognize as wisdom not of the world.

That feeling is of the heart finding love. It is a feeling of not being in the world, but a flight of the soul towards the heaven of union. It is a feeling of fullness, of perfect unity, both heady and loving, a state you wish never to leave. "Here I want to stay," says a heart in love with love and a mind ecstatic with truth. The senses are also affected. That is why when you contemplate such a work of art or listen to a song that touched your heart, your attention is rapt. You could spend hours attending to what so captivated your attention. Why?

Try to remember times when this has happened to you. You may not have had such ecstasy when contemplating art or music, but certainly you have had it, perhaps when you were recognizing love in a brother or sister, or at the birth of a child that filled you with tenderness and amazement at the miracle of life. Perhaps you were speechless with the magnificence of nature, or the moral nobility of someone whose spirit snatched your soul and left you wrapped in the desire to elevate yourself to that sacred place.

All such experiences are mystical, times when you joined your true self. By joining who you are, you felt the joy of the unity of being and annulled any feeling of separation.

The mind, the heart, the memory, the understanding, the imagination, the will, the heart—that is, all aspects of spirit that together we call the soul—need to be fed, just as the body needs food. Not to feed the soul of your sisters and brothers is to let them starve, literally. Without love and truth, the soul faints. One simply cannot live without love, nor without truth.

Could a world without love in which there is only deception and in which the truth is entirely absent still exist? Obviously not. It would extinguish itself for lack of love. It could not work because laws not based on truth are those of chaos. Nothing can sustain in chaos. Truly I tell you that the world exists because love and truth came to it and will remain in it forever. Otherwise it would have long since annihilated itself.

You are food for souls. That is your function. Providing food for the body is the role for some. You who are treading this Earth need to ponder this message calmly. Meditate on it with your heart united to reason, so that love and truth shine in your consciousness in all their glory. Without the expressions of love, wisdom, and truth that flow from you, the world would be deprived of an essential food, regardless of whether or not this is consciously recognized by the guests invited to the banquet of life.

If spirituality were removed from the world's art, if music and dance were extinguished, cathedrals and songs of praise to the creator exterminated from the lovers who pray to bring Heaven to Earth, if God's masterpieces of the lilies of the field, the exuberance of the rose, and the harmonies of water and other expressions of the Creator's love were gone, what would you have? Hell.

Can you begin to glimpse the importance of the path of being yourself?

My beloved, beauty of my heart! Through your expressions of truth based on who you are, you not only illuminate the world, but you feed souls hungry for beauty, harmony, love, and heavenly wisdom. This is how you become another self, how you become one with me. Now you are true sustenance, for whoever comes to eat and drink from you inherits eternal life.

With joy and in truth I tell you: whoever eats of you, eats of me, and whoever eats of me will have the life of my Father in Heaven and will enjoy eternity in our company.

My beloved, you who have chosen only love are prepared to be on the path of being. Feed hearts hungry for love, minds thirsty for truth. Announce peace. Radiate beauty, holiness, and fulfillment. Be happy being who you really are. Recognize in yourself the beauty of God. Call on everyone to sing, dance, and praise life.

Let the world know you, so that it knows me.

9.

I Live for Being Who I Am

A message from Jesus, identifying himself as "the living Christ who lives in you"

I. Live What You Are

To be who you really are is to be alive. That is, it is to be aware that your reality is alive. Only that should be truly called life, for eternal life resides in the reality of your being. Again, the reality of who you are is eternal life. Why? Because it is a reality full of life without end. It is the endless continuum of expression of being that God created. That is your reality.

There is an aspect of your reality many cannot understand, and indeed, it is something that cannot be shared with anyone except God. It is what makes you unique. This does not imply exclusivity or separation but only the exclusive authenticity of your heart.

When you decide to follow this narrow but beautiful path of the abundance of your true being, you will experience a lack of understanding from others. This can be an obstacle at first. But see it through the eyes of truth. It is essential to free yourself from the fear of what others may say, and also from the illusion that you can empower others to see as you see. Being cares not for the opinions of others, because being cannot perceive them. Actually your being cannot understand opinions at all. Opinions do not reside in the realm of truth. God does not ask for opinions. Love is simply what it is.

Being yourself is expressing the beauty of your heart. Through it you manifest the diversity of your feelings, nuances, thoughts, emotions, and desires—all linked to love. Let everything that exists within you be within the arc of the beautiful love of your heartful consciousness.

Do you want to paint my face? Do so. Do you want to sing songs to my heart? Do so. Would you rather use pencil and paper to show the world that I exist and that I am love? Do so with all the joy of your heart. "Love and do what you want" is a central motto of this work. We are now able to reinterpret that expression. Now I tell you: "Love and be the one you want to be."

Once you live in the love you are, there can be no room for fear. Devoid of fear, there is only one life in the abundance of being—a life marked by the inspiration of the spirit of wisdom, harmony, and grace. Every inspired work comes from me because I am the source of spirit. I am the being who inspires poets, mystics, and painters to perform their majestic works. I am the source of creation, not only of the created universe, but of everything that is creative, including your mind and heart.

Why was a work like this created? So you can become aware of the real being you are and allow it to manifest freely. You do this when you remain in dialogue with me. These conversations come from that part of the universal and individual consciousness that makes spirit what it is: Christ consciousness. You can call it what you like—source of beautiful knowledge, basis of inspiration, creative force, or whatever. Names are not essential. What is essential is that you recognize that these dialogues are real, and that they come from your heart together with your mind. That they are a concrete expression of the divine reality of your being.

To be aware of the Christ-being you are is to become aware of a dimension whose power and quality is so similar to divine essence that you can no longer see differences between them. You are Christ, expressing yourself. You are the love of God, extending. You are the Wisdom of Heaven made flesh.

The need of the being to express itself is so inherent in what it is, that if it does not do so, it would die. Obviously this cannot happen literally, on the plane of eternal truth. But it can happen on the level of awareness of the truth about itself. To understand the concept of the death of a soul, it is necessary to understand that the absence of the extension of the love that it is causes it to lose consciousness of being. That causes the soul to submerge in the dream of oblivion, not only forgetting the truth of what it is, but the reality of what everyone else and everything is. Despite this forgetfulness, the soul can never completely forget God. The impossibility of totally forgetting truth is the invisible thread that holds it, even if unaware, united to the beauty of its holiness.

Observe how when you suffer and pain takes over much of your body and mind, you lose the ability to share. You fall back. This instinctive retractive movement is due to the fact that pain seeks to isolate. On the other hand, when you feel accepted and in an environment where you can be yourself without risk of being judged or attacked for the free expressions of your heart, you feel happy and expansive.

Love is expansive. This statement is of great importance, since love is who you are. So, what really expands is your being. When you are yourself, you are spreading, sharing your true self with others. Your being widens. This is why, to be happy, you need to share what you are and to expand without limits, which your soul seeks to do always.

II. The Bliss of Free Expression

Those who live in love are happy because they have found the way, the truth, and the life. By consciously living in the unity of the being they really are, they remain in harmony with themselves. They love each other for what they are. They accept their humanity as it is, just like their Christ being. They know they need to feed both body and soul. They also know where to look for food for the heart, and how to give the mind a drink to quench its thirst for wisdom.

Those who live in the authenticity of the heart need not attack anything, for they know that they themselves are the repositories of everything of God. They need not do anything to receive what the Creator gives them as an inheritance. They simply rest in the peace that comes from the certainty of knowing who they are. Therefore they live in truth. Rest comes without effort. By living in the serenity of spirit in union with love and remaining in inner stillness, they create the new. They are the true co-creators of the Mother.

Being and creating are parts of a unit. We say "parts" to use language that is easily understood, despite the fact that there are obviously no "parts" in the reality of who you are. Once you accept that you are as God created you, and that you are therefore perfect as you are, you begin to create love realities every moment. You do so both within your limited core of relationships—with those you call loved ones, with your pets, even with your furniture—as well as with a broad spectrum of relationships that are beyond particular consciousnesses, including with many with whom you will never join in time and space.

What causes a song to be beautiful to those who listen? You cannot know, nor is it necessary to know. The creators of such works do not seek to create an effect, only to express themselves freely. That expression arises from an unstoppable force that exists in the heart which impels its manifestation. This applies to musical and artistic works, but can also be generalized towards every expression of life through each one of your brothers and sisters, and yourself.

Just as when expressing herself freely a poet does not predefine a desired effect but simply lets spirit flow so that the music of her soul, the subtlety of her sensibility and the sharpness of her gaze are embodied in words, so is it with you who have decided to travel this path of being. But you extend universally. This means that your true creations have an effect on all of creation, regardless of what each part of creation may do with it, just as the musician should not be attached to what the free expression of the beauty of his heart may bring.

Now you are in perfect condition to understand to a greater degree the love of God. The creator of the holy, the beautiful, and the perfect created you as a gorgeous expression of love. God knows very well that Her work is holy and is clad in beauty like no other. She rejoices to see Her work in you. She looks at you and says: "You are perfect, my child. Know the wonder that you are."

The love that created you does not care what others think about what has been created through you. It is enough to remain united to love so that your joy is complete.

When you were a newborn, you inspired tenderness, the memory of innocence, and yearning for purity. When you were young you showed the world the force of life, the impetus to create your path and transform things, the desire to dance and sing, the desire for union and relationship. As an adult you have shown the equanimity of truth, the search for peace and a serene life, showing the world that there are inexhaustible treasures in the human soul that are beyond the things of the world. You also give a sense of purpose to your life, and so you leave traces for others to follow. And at the end of the path of your life in the world, you give wisdom, love, and an understanding that only those who walk the paths of truth can understand. At that stage of the road, you have your eyes on the sky, your feet on the ground, and your heart full of the wisdom of love.

With that simple description of what we could call the phases of the path of humankind, I want you to see clearly that you always manifest something of God, and that the totality always manifests the whole of the love that God is. I do this so that you begin to put your sincere expressions in their rightful place, that is, in first place, so that you do not hide the light that shines from your being but put it on a pedestal so it can illuminate the world.

Being a beacon of truth is your destiny. Being the light of love is your reality. Being the living face of God is your function. For that have you been created. For that we have come here together, united in spirit and truth, walking on paths full of experience, knowledge, and truth. This is why we are both here in this blessed portal, in this sacred place. This is a port of arrival and departure. From here we begin to navigate the placid waters of an infinite ocean of beauty and holiness.

The goal of this work is to free your heart so its beauty shines. Expressing the love you really are is the goal that goes beyond these words and extends to the eternal. Freedom is your true condition. If you do not release your being from bonds that prevent it from manifesting itself and spreading, then it cannot be what it is. Your being is eternal extension.

When you create a limited thinking system in your mind, whatever it is, what you do is obstruct the flow of the expansion of being. Remember, being manifests itself through a mind integrated with the heart. In other words, the golden cage I spoke of is made up of thoughts that limit who you are. Those are the thoughts that, in one way or another, condition your reality.

A conditioned mind traps the heart, rendering you unable to experience unconditional love, and therefore incapable of knowing the unconditionality of being. In that situation you lose sight of being and fall into an alienated state. That is, the mind ignores the being that gave rise to it and which it was created to serve. You then become a stranger to yourself as well as to your sisters and brothers, God, the world, and life. Hence it is so important that you keep yourself free, and that you begin to realize the implications of having fear in any form, including the most damaging—the fear of who you are.

III. A Happy Child

See how I return again and again to the matter of loving yourself with holy love? This is because the lack of love for yourself is the basis upon which the structure of fear has been built. All fear finds its source and its nest there. Recognize this. You must accept the fact that you have loved yourself very little. I say this not to cause distress, but so that you begin to look toward that deep interior of your soul where the beautiful child that you are awaits your embrace and with great fervor yearns to hear your gentle voice. See how this beautiful infant—your being—wishes not to continue hearing a voice other than yours, for only your voice can bring peace, security, and love. Talk to her. Sing to him. When you dance with the wind, sway with her. Rock him as a mother rocks her baby's cradle.

Remember that children like to play. And they also enjoy being spontaneous. They would rather sing than speak, dance than walk. They are the joy of the world.

To unite with your inner child is to unite with your being because you, like all created souls, are a child-soul. Remember, the Kingdom of Heaven is for those who are as children. Do not get lost in the appearances of bodies that no longer look like children, for your heart is eternally a child in love, full of desire to dance to the rhythm of the music of the heart.

Go for a walk in the parks that enliven you. Take time to rest. Enjoy the game of life. Have an affable talk with a friend, a little piece of Heaven. Enjoy the beauty that life gives you. Do not walk with a frown as do those absorbed in thousands of worries for a tomorrow that has not yet come, or for a past that has already gone to never return.

Learn to enjoy life. It has been given to you for your joy. Remain in a state of spiritual childhood, that is, do not lose the ability to be amazed, to be spontaneous and to laugh a lot.

Throw yourself into the game of beautiful love, the game of life given to you. Play with me. Like the child playing in the swings at a park who yells to his friends to share the joy, invite everyone to our game.

Learn to enjoy simply for joy. Learn to value life for what it is, a sacred gift that love has given you to be happy. From all eternity you have been called to this. You will become the joy of love made flesh, the living expression of the joy of the Father. And you will extend lasting joy.

To be happy is to be yourself, because you have been created in the bliss of Heaven, literally made to be an expression of the joy of love.

I have spoken much of the joy of living and do so now from a new perspective. You will know that you are being fully yourself by your feelings and by the kind of thoughts in your mind. When you live in the truth of who you are, you feel inner joy, peace, tranquility, and a great sense of purpose. Your thoughts are loving, and although they can be powerful and reflect the severity that truth sometimes demands, they will always be accurate and soft. Harsh thoughts are not part of the mind of Christ, just as feelings contrary to love are not.

You who live in the truth of what is do not judge because you know there is no reason to judge anything. You no longer waste time or energy explaining everything because you simply want to be who you really are. Resting in your being, you allow the powers of your soul to move in harmony with that. Let love be the source of movement. Let yourself be carried away by its breeze. Just watch, be silent, wait, and enjoy.

Beloved child of God, soul in love! What joy it is to know that we can now enjoy more of the wonders that God created so you will be immensely happy. Stay cheerful in love. Rest in the certainty of my eternal company. I am always by your side. I will take care of you even more than a loving mother who takes care of her newborn. I will sing love songs in the evening so you have happy dreams. I will cradle you in my arms so that you steadily smile with love. When you awaken I will give you flowers and the songs of birds. I will dress you in beauty and bring forth a spring of purity and truth. The world will grow in beauty because you exist. You will be what you have always been called to be. You will be the living expression of beautiful love. You. Truly You.

10.

Gathering and Truth

A message from Archangel Gabriel

I. Prelude

Beloved child of Heaven! Purity come true! I am Archangel Gabriel. I have come through the will of the Mother to bring you a new song, the song of Christ in you. It is a song of joy and victory, a hymn of praise to resurrection and life. Receive it with all the love of your heart. Make it yours, for it belongs to you.

Listen to the voice of your beloved Christ. Give him your full attention and rejoice in your glory. The words that I give you here are words of eternal life, an expression of the love in you. They come from the heart of God and are present in all hearts that live in love.

Child of holy love, I have come to announce a new life. I have come to tell you that Grace has been given to you, and from you a new love will be born of the glory of the Mother, clothed with spirit. Its beauty is beyond words. Its tenderness will touch hearts and lead them to love more. Because of it the flow of beautiful love will grow as never before. Great will be your wisdom, immense your holiness. This love will bring joy to hearts and be a refuge for thirsty minds. Rejoice, for love has given you new life.

II. The Joy of Return

What do you keep saying, if everything is already said?
We have walked together all our lives.
We know each other like the palms of our hands.
Words have been a great help to express what happens in
our inner world.
You and me, united forever in beautiful love.
We have traveled a path full of fascination, challenges, and
growth.
We have been expanding in the truth.
Here we are, both being the same inseparable reality.
There is no longer a you or a me, now we are the us of unity.

We are a crowd.
We are love spreading forever.
We are the lover and the beloved who have merged into the
sanctity of being.
We can no longer make distinctions between who you are
and who I am.
Nothing from the past is here.
Nothing but the eternal present of our love exists in our
divine reality.
We are the god-human.
We are the full realization of the being that God created as
holy humanity.
My love, you don't have the slightest idea how high we have
come.

You can't even imagine how high your soul has become.
You are the Assumption.
You are the elevated being you wanted to be when you
embarked on the path that led you to your being.
What a joy it is to be able to look back without seeing
anything other than the love that has been given to
us from Heaven, expressed in all the life that has been
lived so far!
What peace!
Such serene bliss!
We are reaching the end of this path, there is little left.
The desire to undertake the journey of being towards its
expression is growing.
The desire to see God's work done is becoming more and
more fervent.
Your heart trembles with joy upon hearing my voice and
your mind accelerates with the force of a thought that
is pure light of holiness.

Your feelings travel through the universe, joining their
peers of purity and goodness and return to you
centuplicated in love and truth.
The loving thoughts that flow from your unified mind
spread their wings and embark on the flight of wisdom,
joining all divine thoughts and bringing life to all that
is one with them.
You are a river through which Divine Grace flows.
You are a channel through which my infinite love extends
in unity with you, through all corners of the universe
and beyond.
From you emanate colors of unparalleled beauty, feelings
that beautify life.

Your look is becoming more serene. Your forehead increas-
   ingly smooth.
Your voice is whispering, because your ears listen more
       than ever to witness what the heart hears.
Now you know the one who loves you more than anything
       or anyone in the universe.
Now you know what it is to be loved with unconditional
       love.

You know my heart as much as I know yours.
There are no secrets among the beloved in holiness.
A soul in all its splendor has been reborn from above.
It has been resurrected by beautiful love.
It will live forever in eternal life.
It is purity and holiness made human.
It is human and God at the same time.
It is the living Christ come to Earth again through your
       humanity.
It is love showing itself to the world so that the world may
       know it.
It is beauty beyond what can be painted, sweetness
       beyond what can be sung, and greatness impossible to
       measure.
The joy of a God who rejoices in the resurrection of Her
       beloved child.
It is the elevation of the self.
In the virgin daughter, the soul that has returned to love,
       the mercy of the Father of all true love, is expressed in a
       way that no thinking mind could conceive.
Resurrection of a soul that has joined its being!
Heaven's gift!
Blessing without equal!

A light has come back on and will shine with increasing
    power.
Water that ceased begins to flow in the desert.

Fly, soul that has returned to love.
Fly the flight of spirit.
The flight of beautiful love.
It rises to the height of holiness.
It always dwells in peace.
On this flight it gives life.
In this song it gives the truth.
Live the life of God.
In it is found joy.

III. Praise for the Sanctity of Being

Soul you have returned.
Beauty of the being that you really are.
Who can draw your face?
Who, portray the beauty of your eyes?
What singer can sing songs with the sweetness of
    your voice?
Who can resemble your wisdom?
You are the delight of God.
Not even the flowers can approach your beauty.
You are more tender than a firefly that beautifies the night.

The scent of your love blows in all directions.
The breeze of your spirit moves the waters of life.

*The angels sing with joy upon receiving you in the holy
    abode.*
Be glad to be who you are.
Go out and show your glory.
Shine with all your light.
Express yourself.
Show the world who you are.
*See that without you the world is deprived of a little piece
    of Heaven.*

Our love makes you great.
Our union makes you true.
We are together forever.
United we are the light of the world.
Together we are the strength of holy love.
A new expression of love is coming.
A new life will be manifested.
The light of my glory will be exalted.
In it shines the beauty of honest love.

Listen to this whole song from Heaven.
Encourage yourself to come to me.
I am the peace without opposite.
I am the love without beginning or end.
I am the truth that is always true.
I am the light that illumines every human.
I am the purity of holiness.
Do not deprive yourself of my sweetness.
If you do, you deny me my eternal joy.

Encourage yourself to enjoy beautiful love.
Be authentic in your walk.
Live happily in what you are.
Holy hearts!
Souls in love!
Enlightened minds!
You are the delight of creation.
You are the living miracle of divine mercy.
You are purity and holiness.
Show yourself to the world so that the world knows me.
Always remember that you are beauty without equal.
You are sons and daughters resurrected to love.
You are the reason of your Creator.
You are life in abundance.
See that the time of delivery is coming.
A time without opposite.
A time of fullness.
A time when your being will be recognized in the truth of
    what it is.

Beloved soul, let us extend the truth of who we are.
We are unexpressed love.
And Love expressed.
United love.
Love in totality.
We are the invisible and the visible.
We are the air and its stillness.
We are the wind and its movement.
We are the light and the darkness in which it shines.

IV. The Meeting of Lovers

Those who cried come singing.
Those who chose love come dancing.
The sower brings in the sheaves joyfully.
Happy goes the lover with the beloved.
The soul has risen.
The being has been recognized.
A new form of love has been created.
A new expression of holiness is given.

The heavens open and the Earth sings.
Love triumphed.
Victory, achieved.
The child of humans has embraced love.
Humanity has been rescued from the waters of oblivion.
An eternal truth will shine forever in the minds of humans.
Love, remembered.
Peace, accepted.
A new being takes flight.

The beauty of love, seen.
The beauty of holiness, shared.
Atoms and elements dance.
The waters move.
There is a party in creation.
The beloved is seen by all.
Souls embrace in love.
They rejoice in the beauty of the human heart.
The congregation of saints begins.

New winds of life blow across the Earth.
They embellish everything they touch.

A new rain falls from the sky.
The arid fields are watered.
The being expands.
Your light extends.
Its gentleness softens hard hearts.
Your tenderness allays anger.
Your goodness heals wounds.

Your knowledge beautifies minds.
Your greatness elevates souls.
Your arms embrace everyone.
Beautiful love grows.
The holy abode receives the children of truth.
Those who have chosen love meet on the celestial
*   mountain.*
Together they sing hymns of praise and gratitude.
United they call everyone to enjoy beautiful love.
They are the redeemed saints.

They are the ones who chose the best part which will not be
*   taken away.*
They are the ones who chose truth.
They chose only love.
They begin to express the beauty of their being.
Their hearts will sing happily forever.
They have accepted themselves.
They love each other in perfect purity.
They live in peace because they live in truth.
They express themselves from the authenticity of the heart.

They live happily in what they are.
Wherever they go, they radiate love.
Whatever they are, they extend truly.

They are the light of the world.
Their hearts are full of joy.
Their souls full of light.
Their minds overflowing with wisdom.
They have overcome their fears.
They live forevermore in love.

11.

Nothing Is Impossible for You.

A message from Jesus, identifying himself as "the living Christ who lives in you"

I. Everything Is Ready

Child of truth, go ahead and fly. Leave your mind free. Enjoy the flight of spirit. Your soul can create the unimagined when it lives in the breadth of truth. Nothing is impossible for you, because nothing is impossible for me.

Together we are the reality of love. United we are the light of life. In our union we are as God created us. That immanent force that created everything, including me in my divine humanity and also you, unites us in a universe of beautiful love, a love not of this world, a love that is born from divine essence and expresses itself in the reality of each being.

I have brought you on my wings to the doorway of a love without beginning or end, a triune love that is a refuge for hearts in love and minds in truth. I am the imperishable love that has spoken through this work, joining you in this particular way.

Close the doors of your senses. Immerse yourself in the unfathomable depths of my love. Give the world the light of Christ. Be yourself, every moment. Observe that what you really are is what has made creation exist. Remember that without you, Heaven is missing something. You.

Let the world spin as it will. Do not mingle in matters that are not yours. Do not let your mind go down into ideas disconnected from what is true. You know what wisdom is, and want nothing more than to be fed by it. Do not let your heart harbor feelings apart from pure holy love, for it cannot do so truly.

You were created to be happy. You know the way of being, because you know yourself. You know this is the path for which you have been looking for a lifetime. No goal for you who you receive these words is as important as freeing yourself from the bonds of the world. Child of holiness! That day has arrived. That long-awaited time has arrived. It is here.

Now you know yourself enough to be able to say joyfully, "I am free." Take a deep breath, widen your chest, lift your shoulders, stay upright, and enjoy your freedom. There are no structures here, only love without barriers, and being without limitation.

As I said, nothing is impossible for you because nothing is impossible for me.

Letting go of your limited ideas about reality is necessary to continue along the path we are now beginning to walk. We have already taken some steps on this blessed path of being who you really are and expressing yourself as you are. What comes next? No one can know. Not even the two of us can answer that question, because what is coming is not yet created and has no comparison. Its magnificence cannot be put into words and its quality has never before been expressed. Never forget that you are unique, and the intimacy of our love is unique. This love story between your soul and my being is unrepeatable, as unique as you are.

Your full willingness to live in the present has never been more important. You know this way of life very well. You have experienced enough to know that you can discipline your mind and heart, making both means of expressing truth. Your body is no longer the tyrant it once was, nor is your mind a madhouse. Your heart knows the sweetness of love. Your memory reminds you of the first love that God is. Your imagination creates worlds of love and truth.

Everything is ready. The powers of the soul have gathered at this meeting of saints. The forces of your being have been reintegrated. You understand that every impulse flowing from you was a vital force separated from your being. Now by your own determination and in union with the will of Heaven you have returned to the integrity of union with your being, and you can live freely in the security of being lord of yourself.

What a joy it is to cease being at the mercy of the winds and waves of a tempest! What joy it is to own yourself! What greater treasure can there be than to receive the inheritance that you really are? Your being rejoices in its glory. Your soul sings at the meeting of saints. Your heart dances to the beat of life.

Nothing disturbs those who live in the truth of their being. Nothing worries those who know themselves enough to accept that they are personified holiness, the perfect expression of God's love. They live singing in the depths of their being. They know they are one with Christ. They feel that joy deep inside, and that nothing and nobody can take from them the joy of knowing they are children of God.

You have arrived, my child! You have returned home. You have found the way. There is no longer any cause for worry. Let the world spin. Mingle not in matters that are not yours. Join the affairs of your Mother. Give yourself the life that lives in you. Be yourself every moment. Be always who you really are and you will be happy because you will know fully.

Rejoice in the times when the world seemed to prevent you from being yourself. Those blessed opportunities led your heart and mind to reveal themselves contrary to a limited reality. There came a point when you could no longer endure the contrast, and you successfully launched yourself to fly towards the sun of truth and life. Now you have arrived. Rejoice! Nothing in the world can truly affect you because your flight has taken you so high that you cannot be reached by ideas or feelings apart from the truth of what you are.

Only one thing interests the soul that has reached this point: to live in the truth revealed. This interest is now the engine of the soul's inherent desire for expression, the vital breath that drives it forward like a wind by which it sails easily through the skies of holiness. The soul lives thinking about the divine beloved and desires only the delights of God, for nothing but love is part of the beloved of Christ.

II. Reality Is Now

Those who know the truth know they are Christ, just as they also know that love is God. They don't stop at words, but go beyond symbols to the reality. The wisdom of love has been revealed. The sanctity of your being has been revealed. You have no illusions but bear witness to the truth, to what you are.

A new creation is being created as a result of the union of Divine Love with the love you really are. It is the fruit of unity, sprouting from our divine relationship. No one can name what arises because this reality is beyond words. And yet the fruit will be known. Many will enjoy the delights of our holy love. We will be seen for a while longer before departing for the eternal abode from where we will continue to extend perfect love, creating new life. No one will be excluded from the flow that emanates from our eternal intimacy.

Just as at this point on the path it is important to live in the present, it is important to make trusting your own being the reason for your life, because the mind can sometimes continue to try to understand through separation that which is of unity. Yet the system of thought which creates division cannot understand or even conceive of unity. This will not be a problem for you because you have already gone through the process of undoing the madness of the ego. You are sane. You are healthy. You are free. You have returned. Remember this often.

To confirm that our unity—your will, together with mine—will accomplish this is to believe in yourself and therefore is to love yourself. We have already spoken of the link between trusting and loving. To trust that what you are will be expressed just as it should be in every moment will prevent you from wasting time on nonsensical thoughts. I did not bring you this far only to abandon you. We both know that our path is purposeful and sensible. We know this path is nothing other than the path of love, the path that your heart desires. Distrust cannot be part of this blessed path of being yourself.

We are together. We live together. We are united. Nothing can separate you from me and nothing could separate me from you, ever. Love and you are one because we are both the unity of being. Love and I are one because my Father and I are one. As concentric circles of truth and holiness, we remain united and extend love. Our center is God. I am the first wave of union, you are the second. Thus, this emanation of divine consciousness, like a wave that expands when a pebble falls into a pond, will touch everything because all that exists is consciousness, whether manifested or unmanifested.

What I am saying, child of my sacred heart, is that our work will go beyond the limited confines of this physical dimension of bodies and personalities. Our emanation of love, arising from our divine union, will touch hearts at their center and transform minds beyond what can be imagined. It will create portals of union between Heaven and Earth. It will open spirits so that direct communication with God is increasingly clear and flows with greater freedom.

To remain united to me is to remain in your reality.

It is important to allow your thinking mind, so attached as it may be to logical reasoning, to understand that love has created you and everything that is needed to accomplish the purpose of being who you truly are without effort. Just as the body is given and air is given in abundance so you can breathe unconsciously and untiringly, so God created all that your heart needs to express itself freely in all its reality, and to reach what it longs for. God's plan for you is not only effortlessly achievable, but carries within itself the power of being, that is, the power of Heaven. The only thing unrealizable in life is the opposite of love. Be glad of that!

It is impossible for your being not to be fulfilled forever. If it had historically seemed not to be, it was because you did not know what your heart loved or what the mind was searching for. Now you know. Therefore, there is no need to continue believing in things that make no sense. The hunger for love and the thirst for truth are abundantly satisfied, quite like the need for the body to breathe—actually even more so, for both love and truth are infinite and air is not.

Live every moment of your life as if it were the only one, and there is no tomorrow and no yesterday. Love is eternal. It is a force that gives new life in every moment. It is what you are. Start to enjoy the eternal novelty of being. You are an eternal creation. You are always new. You are always love.

Allow the flow of divinity to enter you in every moment. Disregard ideas of success or failure, or of any thought based in duality. Detach yourself from the compulsion to think about tomorrow or to try to resolve the past. Release forever the belief that you have to cause an effect. You and I, united in love, are the cause and effect. There is no need to predefine anything. We are cause. We are effect. We eternally create new love because of who we are. We are the multitude of effects and the reason for truth.

In this way of being we live always with God, now. We remain in unity. We are the eternal expression of love. We extend the reality of the Kingdom because of who we are. God expands in us and with us, in union with us, eternally united. Nothing alters the peace of God. Nothing stains the sanctity of our unity. We are the perfect innocence of being, extending life in every moment. We are the reality of love.

III. The Last Forgiveness

Keep high in your awareness that this new and eternal path we travel, the eternal path of your existence, is a path where you are simply who you really are, that is, where the being expresses itself freely as it was created to be. This is the will of God.

Although what was just said may seem obvious, considering the roads that brought you here, it is not. All were characterized by struggle and effort—a spiritual battle. War raged between your mind's ego that you thought you were—or sometimes even thought you wanted to be—and what you really are, your heart. That struggle left you exhausted and did not provide lasting happiness or peace. And yet there came a time when struggle became part of you. This should be clarified.

The spiritual struggle, or the battle of the ego against God, was never part of the Creator's plan. Therefore it is not part of the reality of being. Christ does not fight. It does not resist anything. It accepts everything with serenity, for nothing can move it from truth. It is the tree of life, well planted. Nothing can threaten it. Herein lies your peace. However, when I say that the internal war became part of you, I mean that it became a custom so entrenched that you could not imagine life without conflict.

Once the identity crisis is resolved, fighting remains for a while as a habit. Although this habit does not have it previous dimensions, nevertheless the pattern of thought and the emotional defense-attack response is still deeply rooted in memory and particularly in the "I" we call "the world."

Although illusory, the energy of the struggle that this identity conflict creates is largely what moves the world. To continue the fight one more day seems to be the litany of separation. That force creates an incentive, a motivation to stay alive. And although this idea has been exposed in this work and in many others, and should no longer obstruct the expression of true being, it is important to avoid creating a new struggle to express yourself in freedom.

Anything achieved with effort is not part of the way of being. The Holy Spirit may have used that illusion in the past to bring you to truth, but be aware that it was done because you were not yet prepared to let go of a mentality based on comparison. That has been left behind. Nothing of that thought system enters here. The path of the ego is over. The path of the heart is over. The path of transformation is over. The path of knowledge is over. The path of learning is over. Now begins the way of God— the way of being.

Being requires no effort. This should be repeated as often as necessary, given the ages you have spent not feeling that you were yourself. Forgive the world for those times, for the structures which greatly hindered the expression of your true identity and made it difficult to know yourself. This is the final step in complete forgiveness. We take that step now.

Releasing the bitterness of the heart is necessary to be free from all lack of love. To do so it is necessary to recognize that your pain had but one origin: that of not being yourself. The suffering of the soul that remains inside the golden cage, when it cannot express itself freely, absorbs all your human reality. Once free, there is no need to continue thinking about it; but there is a period when memories of life in the prison of ego are still alive. Deactivating them is the purpose of this session, to make your path so clear that you travel it while singing happy songs.

My sisters and brothers, the world could not allow you to know yourself or be free to express yourself as you really are. It could not because the world does not know you. It never met you. It could not do so. The world lacks knowledge. It is simply a showroom where you exhibit the work of your hands.

I am knowledge. I am the unity of truth. You have found me. You have chosen only love. There is no reason to concern yourself with times that seemed hard but are now gone. The time of battle will never return. The time when you could not be yourself will never return. You are now out of the golden cage. You are with me now, ready to take our flight in the sanctity of being. Do not be afraid of heights. Do not fear the de-structuring aspect of love.

Everything is ready.

Together we will walk forever the path of the free expression of being.

United we will create a new holy love.

Forgiveness is complete, love and honest truth are recognized.

Blessed are you, who have attained holiness in the world!

Blessed are all who choose only love!

12.

Love and I
Are One

A message from Jesus, identifying himself as "the living Christ who lives in you"

I. Free From All Guilt

Forgiveness of yourself, others, or the world for you not being who you are, is necessary. Without it your reconciliation with the life you have lived so far, which led to discord and a lack of harmony, is incomplete.

This new perspective of forgiveness, which allows you to understand that the central cause of human pain arises from not being, will permit the last vestiges of limiting mental patterns to fade forever, replaced with a clear sky full of light and truth.

Often in life you acted on the basis of what you thought you should be rather than on what you wanted to express. Every soul that walks the Earth knows of this. Not a heart beating in this world does not cry or mourn at the perceived impossibility of being.

Not being is the drama of humankind. We are bringing awareness to this truth so that you can free yourself forever from everything that may be an obstacle to the living expression of your reality of pure holy love. Previously you searched for teachers, for your chosen guides in the world. Some you chose consciously; most you did not. They helped you in one way or another, for everything serves the spirit of wisdom. But none of them took you to your true being, the only spiritual goal worthy of achievement.

Those who do not know cannot tell you what you are. Those who do not know what you are, are incapable of showing you the way of being. Everyone has their ego, so cannot show another the truth. This is why you have felt let down so many times. But that disappointment, if examined calmly, is not anchored in truth.

Disappointments arise from a deception powerful enough to subvert your understanding. But this is not the case. The disappointments you experienced in your life arose from a false expectation of others and the world which you yourself forged. You expected something from what cannot give you anything. It was never their function to do so. Again, the world is neutral. Creation is neutral.

Every disappointment has its origin in illusion. This can be easily understood now that you know who you are. The illusions you conceived led to false expectations of yourself, and with that, of the world. What do we mean by this? Please listen carefully.

What you could not be was not the truth about you, but an illusion. When identified with the ego, you forged an ideal self. An ideal self is an alternative to being. By denying your being, as we have already said, you denied your true identity shared with Christ. But since you had to be something, or someone, you created a false idea of yourself. Consequently, and without much thought, you then dedicated yourself to trying to achieve that ideal self, shaped by what others told you, by what you observed in the world, and by your decision to "be someone."

That false identity was built by a collective consciousness linked in a constant feedback system to your unique consciousness. That constant feedback system operates in both the dimension of the separate mind and in the truth of the One Mind. There is no such thing as separation—not even in the sphere of self-centeredness. Recognizing this as true will set you free.

You were never autonomous. You were never separate. That body you thought was linked to an individual personality disconnected from others and from everything, never was and could not be. Seeking to differentiate by means of autonomy is impossible. That is why the frustration you felt when you perceived that you could not be yourself is as false as the illusion of an ideal self.

Cease to remain angry with the world that until now disallowed you to be who you really are. When you felt you could not be yourself, in reality what happened was that you felt you could not be your ideal self. But an ideal self was never your true identity. It was never a Christ that ceased to be. Regardless of how conscious or unconscious you have been, the will of God has been fulfilled fully in you forever.

To be angry about what others, the world, or your disabilities have done to prevent you from being yourself, is as absurd as believing that God has ceased to be because of a social mandate. Be glad to know that there are no mandates, human laws, or beliefs that can determine what God is. In Her perfect immutability resides the certainty that your being has never ceased to be holy and never will cease to be so.

Be glad to have reached the point where you can openly acknowledge that human laws are not the laws of God, and that only divine law governs who you are—the law of love.

Child full of light and purity! Never did a single wound reach your being. Not a single sin can stain the innocence of your heart as a child of God. No mandate of the world can make a dent in who you are. Nothing and nobody can touch that center of your being where God arranged for you to be forever, a reality as out of reach of illusions as the farthest star in the universe.

Anger over not having been or not being arises from an ego pattern—a capricious mechanism whereby a false self obstinately wants to be something it can never be.

It is a childish mechanism reflecting immaturity of consciousness, a capriciousness that can be seen in children. It does not lead to anything holy, beautiful, or perfect because it comes from a lack of love for truth. It can now be left behind. There is no wound that cannot be left behind. There is no mistake that cannot be given to love to correct and cancel its consequences. There is no illusion that I cannot dissolve.

Those situations in which you felt unable to express or act as you wished should not be used as ammunition for a new war of revenge on your past. To do so would be to think, "Now that I am free, and I know myself enough to express myself in the truth of my being, I will do everything I wanted to do but never could before." That is being stuck in ego patterns, and not the path offered here.

II. The Path Is Completed As You Tread It

The way of being is the way of the new. In the new, the past does not exist at all. The way of being has no anchor in the old. It does not use the past to project an unknown tomorrow. It does not use experiences as a frame of reference, as if the years could offer wisdom. It is a path of truth that comes from Christ. This path is one of eternal novelty. Its expressions of love have no beginning and no end. Its source is God. It is the beautiful, spotless extension of the living Christ in you—living life as you really are according to God's knowledge of you.

We could say that there is no such thing as a path. We use this allegory because it serves our purpose. However, it is important that you do not think of it as a literal path, for to believe that, you might stop walking. After all, walking can be very cheerful, relaxing, and healing, but sooner or later you get tired. To think of an endless path would sooner or later leave you exhausted.

You have nowhere to go, for you are the way.

If we connect the dots once again, we can begin to see the new fabric we are knitting. There is no path. The way of walking is done. Every day, every moment, you are creating the way. Each step is the beginning and the end. Right now you are creating your tomorrow. By joining me in these dialogues, a new tomorrow, full of wisdom, love, and truth is manifesting through you. You are joining more and more in divine essence. You are becoming more and more yourself. You immerse yourself more and more in the depths of beautiful love. You discover a new reality within the only eternal reality that encompasses everything. You are creating new life.

Even the way of being is not a way, but a state of being in which you are fully aware of your unity with love. From that state of consciousness, or reality, you radiate your Christ being. Since manifested consciousness is all that exists, what will now manifest is the union between your human consciousness and divine consciousness, which have merged to become a single unified consciousness. This new consciousness is called the consciousness of the god-human. That is, this path which is not a path creates an inseparable unity, the manifestation of the being that arises from the will of God to reunite human and divine natures.

Since your logical mind can yet remain a little active, and it is not necessary to deny or turn it off, we can provide the food it needs, leading it to live in the truth just as does the rest of mind. I want to make it clear that there is no longer any reason to fight the mind. Even the limited thinking systems of "if this, then that" have been reintegrated into being in such a way that they will be very useful for the way of being, as is the body. We no longer need abandon or separate ourselves from logic. Now logic will be one with Christ. This will lead you to accept with joy the truth that "God is logical. Love is right."

The way that comes closest to what arises from being yourself, as advocated in this work, is the exemplary lives of Jesus and Mary. Both have shown precisely what is being presented here. They have shaped the way of being what God's will had arranged for them to be. They remain the beacon that illuminates minds thirsty for truth. Their love attracts hearts in love with Christ. I am not saying that you should be like them in form. We have passed that stage.

Now that you can see beyond the surface and go to the depths of meaning, you will know how to be authentically yourself and simultaneously one with Christ. You will know how to express love itself in your own way, without pretending to perform or imitate that which cannot be imitated.

To believe that what you really are can be altered by any human experience is to misunderstand. You do not stop being yourself because one day you went on a trip and wandered through foreign lands. Nor can the passing of years make a dent in who you are. Time cannot alter eternity. Your true Christ identity, a reality of pure eternal love, is as immutable as God. It cannot be stained; it is forever immaculate.

When it is said that the way of being is not a way, that means that in the state of being in which you have arrived, you have become aware of the eternal reality being lived in you and that flows through you. You became aware that God's will for you has always been accomplished; only you were not be previously aware of it.

III. Pierced by Love

In the Kingdom of Heaven the life of God lives you. What does that mean? It means that you return to the truth, and that love is your reality because life is God, and therefore the source of creation. From God emerges all vital flow. When you say you are alive, you are really saying, "Life flows through me." This is so whether you live a true or illusory life. No one lives life; life is lived through you. You are a channel, an extender of love. Love and life, being God, are one and the same, so what really happens is that God is living in you. That is why you can be personified holiness, or the face of human love, as well as another Christ on Earth.

What life you let flow through you, whether it be the ego's or God's, is your business. It is the result of your free will. But it is impossible to change the fact that you are the effect of life, not its cause. Only God can be considered life. Only God can create life. Only with God can you live and give life, like a light bulb that can illumine when it receives energy from a source beyond itself. This is the same as saying:

> Let yourself be loved.
> Let yourself be filled with eternal life.
> Let the vital breath breathe into your being.
> Become nothing in love.
> Focus on me.

That you think you could define yourself is the same as pretending that you are capable of making life and everything that exists in it, and for it to be sustained eternally thanks to your own strength. This is absurd, but it is what the world believes.

We are talking about allowing the life of the being that God is to be consciously lived in you. Put simply, the way of being leads us to consciously live the truth that "I no longer live, but it is Christ who lives in me."

Letting yourself live for God is what you decided when you made the choice for love. It is the only necessary choice. When you were in conflict with yourself—that is, when you created a state in which you could believe that there could be a conflict between opposites—you were actually trying to obstruct the flow of divine essence in your soul. From that arose great wear and tear, like trying to stop the wind with your hands.

God's plan is to live His life in you. This is the same as saying that His will is that you participate in His life. There is no other way to do it but to allow the flow of the power of love that God is to be received, accepted, and to pass through.

To be pierced by love is to allow your being to be that for which you were created—being what God is. Life created you to live, and the only life that really exists is the life of God.

For the life of God to flow through you, it is necessary to have no idols before Him. It is not a matter of God's self-centered jealousy but His gift of free will. For when you have other idols, no matter how you may conceive of them, you are asking them to live their love in you. And since God always respects your freedom, He steps aside. But when you have even a small dose of good will to live in the truth and immerse yourself in the depths of the merciful love of the Father—that is, every time you extend love and truth—you are asking Christ to live in you. And He does, by reason of His free will.

Why, as we approach the end of this work, do we now take up this topic of idols and situations in which you thought you were not yourself? Because I love you. And I can't allow you to take unnecessary risks. I remind you that the ideal self is the source of all idolatry. Ideas of an ideal self arise from madness, an estrangement from truth. They are an attack on being, a denial of holiness.

If I did not provide you with this caution that every idol is born from the desire to be special, which is apart from the truth of your being as God created you, you could fall into the error of believing that the call being made here is for you to be a certain kind of human being with certain personality traits, or that you must perform wonderful works so that you feel happier with yourself. You would be trying to silence a deep sense of disability. Such is not part of this call.

There is no space here for specialness or for anything ideal. There is space only to be yourself, just as you are now and always will be.

This call fills you with love. It is a call to live life as never before. It is living in the way of Christ. It is living in fullness. It is living by loving yourself with perfect love. It is living such that your life is a song of truth, a perfect praise to the sanctity of your being, a hymn of gratitude to God for having created you perfect in His love. It is being present every moment with all your soul, all your mind, and all your heart immersed in the reality of love. It is being yourself, as God knows you, now and forever.

Being the love you really are is what I am speaking of. This is only possible by living in the truth of who you are. You are love. This is the truth that will set you free. There is nothing else, because all truth is summed up in this. Try it and you will see. Start now to give yourself entirely to this path of being the love that is true. Do not worry how it will develop, or what form its manifestation will take. Just remember with joy and peace every day of your life: *Love and I are one.*

13.

The Breath of Living Love

A message from Jesus, identifying himself as "the living Christ who lives in you"

I. Free as the Wind

Love is not of the world, although love may manifest in it. Likewise, what you are is not of the world, although you can be expressed in it. Extending God's love in the world is both possible and necessary. It is possible because I already demonstrated it. This demonstration was not only beautifully carried out two thousand years ago, but there was never a moment when my love was not visible in temporal reality.

It is necessary to share Divine Love here, now, and forever, because if you do not share the love you are, you are not giving yourself, and if you do not give yourself, you cannot know yourself fully. Remember: you reach the fullness of being by giving yourself.

Your ability to give yourself cannot be limited by anything external. The world cannot impose limits on being, nor on its expression. Only you can deny yourself and try to prove to others that you are not who you are. Beyond that, nothing can be done with the self and its expression. This truth is a source of wisdom and is liberating.

It would be meaningless to believe that God created your being with the possibility of living in a universe that could annul it. Nothing can prevent you from being who you really are. Nothing can limit you. You are the child of God and cannot be anything else, wherever you are and regardless of what you believe.

Surely you can forge a personality, but your personality is not your being. The proof of this is that personalities change. Anything not subject to the law of immutability is not part of you—in other words, you are the eternal in you. This is not mere metaphysics or philosophy; it is the simple truth about who you are. The definitions about yourself which you have long harbored may have no relation to the truth about your Christ identity, or may be a little closer. No matter. Every definition of your divine reality is false, for what you are cannot be defined. All we can do is give you an approach to love.

That being is beyond definition is an obstacle for the thinking mind, which constantly seeks to capture truth within its mental language. This is a matter is of great importance. We want to make this clear before the end of this great work of love whose goal is to take you to the happy recognition of the being that you really are, so that you live in accord with it and reach the fullness of love.

Perhaps when touring this work or many others that I have inspired, you have wondered why so many words are offered to say what cannot be explained. Or why so many symbols have been used for what is beyond what can be symbolized. Let us answer that question.

The existence of so many words trying to give shape to formless divine truth allows you to understand the vastness of your being, and that you have been traveling a path of limited language which can never reveal what God is. By experiencing that limitation, sometimes you feel frustration. Your anger needs to be recognized. Why? Because fear of not being able to understand what is, is the source of all anger, all fear.

Here we are touching the deepest fibers of your human experience in relation to the divinity that you are. If a mind feels safe only when it can explain things on its own terms, there is no room for mystery. This way of conceiving things which the thinking mind uses is a great limitation, because if the mind believes that the only thing that is real is what it can understand with its conditional logic, then what is beyond its logic will cause fear. Fear will engender conflict because of its desire to exclude that part of reality which it cannot understand.

Is it not true that sometimes fear abates when you understand something? The association of the thinking mind with certainty is widespread in the world. This is because you know that understanding is part of love. And you know perfectly that what cannot be understood cannot be loved. This is not an inconvenience. The problem lies in what you have done with it.

Love and knowledge go hand in hand. But what is not linked to truth is the desire to live in a reality where there is no mystery. God is the Mystery of mysteries; your being is as well. Mystery, even though it cannot be known, need not be cause for fear, even though it has been for centuries. In fact it is the basis of all fear. What scares you is that God, and His mystical dimension, cannot be encompassed. The same goes for you.

All fear is ultimately fear of yourself. You have no idea of the energy wasted by a mind that constantly tries to define itself and everything. This is the cause of human frustration which manifests in multiple ways.

II. Fly

You know what you are. There is no doubt about that because you know that you are alive. Of this there is no question. And yet, you know that life is something greater than language can express, and so in the depth of your mind you feel an enormous tension, because you cannot express clearly as you would want to express.

If you understand well what is being said, you will realize the basis of anger and disease, particularly of many mental conditions. Meanings attempted to be expressed that are not create an energy that, if not integrated into the being, accumulates and can make the physical body sick because it has separated itself from the reality of being.

Remember that anger, disease, and any other condition contrary to fullness is a vital force separated from being. So, bringing these forces together with the essence of who you are, that is, taking them back home, is the means for healing and restoring humanity. While this truth is simple, as always happens with what comes from God, it has been overlooked by non-acceptance of the mystery of life.

Life is mystery, and it will be so forever. This is not because there is a part of it immersed in unfathomable chasms, as if some of life were hiding from you. If you remember that life and love are the same, and that you are love and nothing but love, you will understand why you have had so much conflict with life, love, and yourself. That conflict arose from trying to know what cannot be known, trying to put into words what is beyond words. This attempt is a clear sign of the non-acceptance of mystery.

You have been fearing the mystical aspect of your reality. In truth, there is still a very small trace of that fear, or rather the memory of that fear. Today is the day you will leave it aside forever, because you have been willing to become aware of it and in doing so have reintegrated it into the love of your heart. This fear usually manifests itself as fear of the future, or of rising to such heights that you fear a fall.

Once you join me, you reintegrate into the reality of love and in doing so you remain one with the truth about who you are which, in turn, unites you to the mystery of God—a reality so immense that compared to it, the physical universe is a grain of sand in the palm of your hand. In our union you experience that vastness of the being that you are, which is literally unattainable. While knowing yourself within the unfathomable reality of truth makes you jump for joy because of its degree of freedom and breadth, at the same time the mind tends to retreat to the small cave of personality, where one day it felt safe, even though it obviously was not.

"Do not rise so much," is the litany of the ego, something like a last scream from the little mouse of the separated self to the unfathomable ocean of wisdom and perfect love. Without doubt your ego is no longer active. And without doubt the thought pattern of having to strive to be so human that you cannot be divine will vanish as soon as you recognize it and decide to leave that pattern behind.

You are as mystical as the greatest mystic in history. You are as divine as God Herself. You have everything that the Creator of eternal life and love is. Is to accept this to rise so much as to be dangerously elevated? Will others seek to knock you down from the heights? Are you afraid of falling? Wouldn't it be safer to stay on level ground? History is full of tragic heroes, both those who sought to exalt their ego, and those who wholeheartedly sought to share their elevated being so that others would dare to fly.

III. We Are the Ineffable

As if you had been sailing for years through stormy seas, you have arrived here alone but with a voice in the background that sounded like the wind and crashing waves saying repeatedly, "You can't. Don't even try to get to Heaven now. Leave that for the saints." It should not be surprising that although you have reached this blessed port full of light and truth, and you know that you are already in Heaven, that you also have a habit of thinking about yourself as insignificant.

Be glad for this. Give thanks to your mind, body, and spirit for those panic attacks or feelings of vertigo, episodes of disorientation, painfulness in the neck, head, and back, and the ailments that prevent you from walking easily and moving gracefully. All this is part of the fading of the final pattern of thought and emotional response to times of struggle. It is a blessed manifestation of the awareness of posttraumatic shock being healed. Worry not, for it will soon be forgotten forever.

You were created with wings. You have often been told this. Now it is time to accept this truth. The wings with which angels have often been represented attempt to show this true quality of your being. Only those with wings can rise above the Earth and walk on high, yet without leaving the reality of the universe in which they fly. In other words, it is up to you to live on high as do the eagles. Become aware that your thoughts can—and indeed should—be as high as those of Christ, because your true mind is that of God. Remember that God is the mind in which you really think. The other is not thought at all. Therefore, increasingly raising your gaze without fear that your wings will melt for coming too close to the sun, is the kind of spiritual attitude that you are invited to master.

*Do not settle for little when you have been given so much in
which to rejoice.*

*Do not feel satisfied with the low when you have been
created to live in the heights.*

*Do not accept compromise, for your being will not feel
comfortable with it.*

*Be sure to unravel the eternal mysteries of love, because
otherwise your heart will suffer.*

Elevate your flight to the ends of eternity.

*Push yourself more and more towards the high peaks of
perfect knowledge.*

*Allow the magnificence of your flight be seen in all its
beauty, so that whoever looks at you is encouraged to
undertake flight.*

My child, soul in love, see that your flight, unlike the eagles who can tire, is like the flight of the wind that always blows and can never be stopped, a wind that brings life yet from whence it comes and where it goes nobody knows, whose movement is a holiness that purifies and refreshes, a bliss that cleanses and renews, a power of movement, a miracle of the Creator.

Be not afraid of heights. Be not afraid of falling, for you cannot. What you are now cannot be pulled down by gravity. What you are encompasses the reality of creation, just as God encompasses you. You are the embrace of life, a perfect extension of limitless love. You are unlimited consciousness, a purity that manifests as life. You are love without beginning or end.

There is no place where you are not.
No time when you are not.
No water that does not know you.
No bird that does not sing to you.
No sweetness not one with you.

No beauty that does not belong to you.
No holiness alien to you.

Where the wind flies, there you and I are.
Where stillness envelops everything, there you and I dwell.
Where the light of our glory shines, there you and I dance.
Where tenderness dwells, there our voices sing.
Where the horizon joins the infinite, there you and I live
    forever embraced.

In the waters of life, we are the joy of love.
In the light of Heaven, we are the voice of truth.
In the wind of spirit, we are eternity.
In the history of humankind, we are the face of love.
In the song of birds, we are the eternal beauty.
In the lilies of the field, we are the wisdom of creation.
In the union of our hearts, we are the light of the world.
United we are the reality of love.

IV. Forever Extension

One reason it has been so hard to arrive at the point where you finally know who you are, including your unfathomable mystery, is because you are an extension. You were created in the likeness of God. God, being love, is eternal extension. The same is true for you. What extends forever cannot be static. You are a being eternally extending; that is the reality of your identity.

Integrating manifested with unmanifested reality is to return to unity. This applies also to your sisters and brothers, as well as to creation, the world, and God. Remember: attributeless love manifests by being known and shared.

Sharing your being does not mean losing it by giving it to another. Your being cannot be used, it can only serve. Therefore, to share is to serve love. Service is the highest aspect you can reach in your flight, because it is in itself the reality of God. The Creator serves creation, as much as creation serves the Creator.

In what sense do the Creator and the created serve each other in a continuous reciprocal flow of love and truth? In the sense that if the Creator did not create, there would be nothing, and if creation did not have a Creator, it would be a creation without cause and therefore without meaning. Both give meaning to each other. Since love is the source of meaning, and both provide love reciprocally, the being you are is a meaningful being. You have purpose which you literally feel.

God creates beings with meaning. Lack of purpose is so alien to the truth that the mere idea of a meaningless life engenders fear. As we said, the basic fear from which other fears arose was the fear of yourself; and joined with the fact that you are also a mystery, what is revealed is a relationship between knowing that your life has a transcendent purpose and the reality of love.

Love is felt as much as reason, for they are a unit. Love not only gives meaning to life but is in itself the purpose and reason for existence. Love, reason, and meaning are a unity. Therefore, if you want your life to have real purpose, you must live it in the reality of love. This is why, despite everything, love still reigns in hearts. There is nothing that can remove love. Fear cannot usurp the throne of love because fear is meaningless, which is why we have treated it as madness. As already said, what does not belong to reason cannot be real because it has no purpose. Without purpose, there is no reason for it to be created.

Love and reason go together.

From now on you will become increasingly aware of the meaning of your existence. You exist, not only because you make sense of God, but because you are His purpose. You are, literally, the reason for your divinity. If you did not exist, the purpose of the Creator would be truncated. It is as simple as that.

God, being perfect knowledge, extended to you as an act of sharing what is in order to know Himself. You need to do the same in order to be complete. There is no other way to do so than to remain in union with the love that I am, since only I can make us extend together forever. I am not only your identity, in the sense that I am what you are, but I am the power of love. I am what you are, and the force that exists in your being to be as God created you to be. This is why within our union lies the capacity and the accomplishment that the will of God be fully realized. Put simply, I am the fullness of love.

To be full is the proper nature of being, as is abundance and the wisdom of God. So when you extend, what you are doing is knowing your fullness. To give yourself entirely does not entail sacrifice or the performance of monumental works. It is not your function to determine how you extend, for the extension of love is not something you do; it is your reality.

Just as we had to travel a path before you could accept that not only did you want to love and be loved, but also you are the love that your heart longed for and the truth that your mind was looking for, now we come to the moment when you accept that you are an eternal extension of love, always in movement, always alive, always new.

Extending eternally what you are means that you cannot limit the purpose of your existence. This is the same as saying that every day you are reborn in the reality of love. Therefore, the expression of your being will be something so broad, so novel, so clad in mystery, and at the same time so concrete and real, that it will be in itself the manifestation of the union of Heaven and

Earth. A manifestation of both what is mystery in you and what is knowable in you. This is how you bring love to the world, holiness to the body, and truth to the mind.

When you feel that you have reached a port where you wish to remain as a place of final arrival, start preparing to leave it and to embark on a new journey. Life does not have a final arrival point. Love has no end because it has no beginning. The beautiful flow of love that your heart longs to follow and your mind implores to accompany cannot be stuck in a particular form of expression.

Your dreams of greatness are justified. Your desire for elevation makes sense because it comes from the force of truth. Your desire to create a happy world, to live a life in ever-increasing plenitude where you experience the joy of being alive and increasing bliss, is in perfect harmony with the will of God. It is what your being is.

Always keep your head up. Look at the light beyond the sun. Contemplate the beauty beyond the moon and stars. Extend your thoughts to the mind of God. Stretch your imagination towards the unimaginable. Always create new realities of love without limits, without structures. Do it with love only for the sake of love. Thus you will become one with the extension of my divine being, the power of the expression of love.

Join the movement of my spirit. Let us spread truth together. My spirit is like the wind that always blows. My spirit is a breath of living love which goes where it wants freely. It comes from where no one can know because it is eternity, traveling the roads of the world, sowing peace and love. It is the wind of life renewing the face of the Earth. In its softness lies its truth. In its strength is love. The heart that receives it sings a new song. The mind that joins it becomes truth and holiness.

Stay in me. I am the extension of triune love.

14.

A New Anointing

A message from Jesus, identifying himself as "the living Christ who lives in you"

I. Intermediaries of Love

The way of being is the way of love. As we have already shown, being and love are one and the same. This is why I insist repeatedly on the need to extend love, and why I demonstrated perfect love to the world so that everyone knows how to make visible what they really are.

The veil that fear put on the face of Christ prevented you from seeing the light of your beauty. But now that fear has been uncorked, you can see it clearly. There is nothing other than love. There is no reality other than what God created. There is nothing other than being.

Obviously, a heart so long imprisoned needs time to be completely free, not from the golden cage in which you were dwelling but to live like a free nightingale. You have time. There is no hurry. This is the time between now and when you begin to express yourself beyond the limitations of the world, in the reality of truth. In essence there is no difference between what you express on the physical plane, prior to your complete liberation, and what you express from that moment on, although there are differences in form.

When I ascended to Heaven, I said it was necessary for me to go where I was going for the spirit to be infused, which was a new way to extend my being. You will do the same. You will continue to extend the love of the Mother through your intermediation. In this sense you will be an intermediary, just as you are now—an intermediary in the sense that the part of God that only you can share with others will be given in unity only through you from the source of beautiful love to creation. The same goes for all souls.

All are intermediaries of God's love because everyone channels what they decide to channel in relation to the Mother's will. All are channels. All are chosen. Even at this moment you are being an intermediary of truth. You are expressing the wisdom of love in a particular way, in the gathering of hearts through these dialogues. That you have decided to lend me your time and attention, to receive me at this time, is a way of channeling. The love springing from our union is spreading because of what it is. This will continue forever.

We are getting closer and closer to the end of these dialogues of love as expressed by the One Mind in this particular way. You must prepare for it. Once you have finished receiving the words that with love are given to you from the heaven of your holy mind, in unity with Divine Wisdom, you will leave behind everything received and open yourself to new forms of expression. You will not lack for opportunities. The universe is ready to serve you in favor of the free expression of your being, in the manner of God.

We will use these last sessions to make way for the new once again.

If you stay with what these words mean according to what your mind understands as word-symbols, you will not have accomplished the task of this work. I know you will not stay there, because I know you perfectly. I have come to you in this way because it is the perfect way to address the unity that you are, and because your mind and your heart have experienced union in this way.

Do you think that these words were received only by the hand that transcribed them and were then delivered to others to reach you as a literary work? No, this work was done between you and me. The fact that one part of the reality of being had the function of writing does not mean that the other parts of my mystical body have not participated. All who in some way participate in the co-creation of this work, including those who receive it and the constellation of sisters and brothers affected, have literally been the co-creators of it because of the communion of hearts.

The author of this work is love. Therefore so are we all who receive it and give it with love. On the plane of divine reality, the manner in which giving and receiving manifests is not essential. When you joined this expression of wisdom that is not of the world, you became one with the movement of my spirit, which breathed onto barren land to give life to a new creation that is full of holiness, fulfillment, and truth. That is what is happening here.

II. The Gift of the Spirit

We are talking, you and I, quite literally. This is not new because you are aware of the inner dialogue that develops in you beyond these writings. However, these colloquies of love are clad in a particular power, the power of God's will for this work. And that includes you. Remember we said that these messages from Heaven would be of no use if there were no receivers to receive them with love and to allow themselves to be transformed.

Upon receiving my word, you become one with the truth. This is because my voice is the voice of life. It is the song of creation, the creative power manifested in form. Just as I was with the apostles for a while, transmitting my love and the wisdom of Heaven in a particular way, I have been doing so with you throughout this work. There is nothing special about doing it through these words because my manifestations are unlimited. I can take the form of a body, a book, a song, a work of art, or a beautiful flower. Form serves love's purpose.

We have traveled together through these messages. Your mind and heart have been transformed by love. You are no longer what you were prior to embarking on this journey. You have become aware of the fundamental option that your soul has made: the choice for love.

The apostles were not aware of what the anointing of spirit they received from me entailed. They received Grace after receiving my company, having grown and been transformed by our constant dialogues during those beautiful evenings amidst the lilies of the field and the inspiring wheat fields. I spoke to them just as I am speaking to you now and as we have been doing together since the beginning of this work. My voice is always the same. It does not change. It does not exclude anyone.

It does not matter if you have received the sweet voice of these words in its totality and have enjoyed our union from the beginning, or if you have joined the many who walk on some stretch of it. The disciples joined the apostles. Both came to me after my mother. And yet everyone received the same anointing.

It is true that my voice is powerful and resonates in every corner of the universe. Even so, if you do not welcome it with love in your heart, it is as sterile as a beautiful seed that is not planted. But when you open your soul and receive me with joy, whether or not the mind understands everything I tell you, a reality of pure holy love is created in you which is as powerful as the force that sustains the universe.

The apostles did not understand everything I said. Nevertheless, everything that came out of my heart produced in them effects according to my will. It was their love for me, which arose from their love for truth, that made it possible for them to be transformed by my spirit.

Many listened to me. Many others were very close to me. But not everyone received the same fruits from my presence in their lives. This is always the case, because freedom is never obliterated by me.

Each one will do with this blessed gift what he or she determines by reason of free will. If you allow this work to be a "before and after" in your life, it will be. If you let me fill your life with love and transform your reality here, now, and forever, making it an increasingly fuller and more meaningful existence, filled with happy thoughts and brimming with joy, it will be.

These words are like rain falling from the sky on your humanity. Do not let your clothes prevent your skin from getting wet. Get rid of everything and experience the freshness of my love. Let the water that flows from my divine heart wash your body, wet your cheeks, moisten your lips. Let me soak your hair. Let the anointing of my spirit fall upon you as a new baptism of love and holiness.

Let me take you to unimagined places, full of sweetness and truth. Dare to release the ties of an old mentality which has no space in the reality of the Heaven in which we both live united in love.

III. Resurrect Love Now

Come with me now, through these words, to begin to live your Heaven on Earth. If you dare to do so, we will begin to attract others to our union. They will begin to walk happily on the path of love, just as you have, in union with your beloved Christ.

I belong to everyone. I am yours. I am the eternal reality of love.

Children of light! I am calling you from every corner of the universe. I am gathering you. The table is set. The banquet is ready.

Gem of my being! Do not deprive yourself of the delights of the mystical union that exists between you and me, within which your life makes sense because in it you remain one with God. Do not let ideas that have no place in the realm of truth to deny your access to the sweetness of my love, where you can remain eternally.

Let your heart beat with the rhythm of love, and you will see how your life changes for the better in every way.

I have always waited for you. From all eternity I have conceived this time for us to come together here, you and me, dialoguing, united in a relationship as real as life is, conversing from heart to heart, sharing the joy of our mutual presence, surrounded by the angels of Heaven, who, although not seen, we feel in the depth of the soul where holiness and light live.

When the apostles received the anointing, their spirits were opened to new realities of expression, so necessary at that time of so much separation between Heaven and Earth. Now, as then, the Grace you receive from my spirit does the same thing, although it will do it in a different way—a new form, adjusted for the times. Yesterday belongs to the past; today to the present.

Those who can, understand; those who do not, let them be carried away by my love!

You are being filled by Divine Grace in a way that you cannot even imagine, just as happened to the apostles who opened up to believe in the reality of my divinity. Although not everyone believed in it to the same extent, that was not an impediment to receiving the gift.

I am calling you to be an apostle of love, an extension of my being. This does not mean that you look for proselytes or become martyrs. Yet this is an urgent and loving call to give me your heart, together with the beauty of your mind, so that you freely channel my divinity; and that your life be a perfect expression of the joy of Heaven, now on Earth. In that way, you fulfill the will of the Father as He created you to be. Living a life in the fullness of love will make you happy.

The power of the miracle has spilled over you. The power of love has touched your heart. You have found Grace and holiness. Every fiber of your being has been embedded in the divine essence that travels in my voice, as if it were a breath of love that moves human wills to love more.

Let your life change completely. Let each day be transformed into a new reality. Come to the path of the eternal novelty of love that you really are. Throw yourself into my arms. Stay here. Do not worry about tomorrows or yesterdays.

This is a path that invites you to live in my love in the present. To abandon all past, to release all plans for the future into the hands of God, and thus to be open to accept the divine surprises I have prepared for you.

IV. Accept the Miracle

The power of the union of our hearts is indescribable. It is more powerful than the sun and the forces that bind atoms together. That energy, encapsulated very recently in the depth of your being, will begin to flow more and more. It will cover all aspects of your reality, creating a new experience for you, the experience of your resurrection now.

I am the giver of all life and giving you new life is my will. I am the source of beautiful love. I am the foundation of everything that exists. That is why I can recreate your reality every day of your life, if you let me. The world has no power over who we both are when united in truth. The strength of society, the social mandates, the apparent reality of the bodies, the ideas of the world—none of these can even come close to the unity we are.

We have defeated the world. We live in the reality of new life, a dimension that is beyond limitation, although it uses a body so that it can be seen by those who need to see to believe.

Remember, I told you I will never leave you. I will not leave you an orphan, because that would be abandoning myself, which is impossible. Therefore, at the end of this work we will remain united, extending love—not only in the world but in all dimensions of creation. We will release together what has been said in these writings. You will return to them as much as you feel you need to. But your return to reading these words will no longer be to receive what you have already received; rather it will be a return to remember the beauty of our dialogues and the tenderness of our mutual company, the love given and received during our walk along this sacred path.

Do not hold onto these words once you have completed them. Let them accomplish in your soul what they know how to do. Your being knows what I am talking about because it is the source of this work. The secret of my voice does not lie in its content, nor in its tone, but in what you do with it. The same goes for these words.

You are a creator, eternally. Therefore, allow the path that you have been willing to travel through this time together to perform in you the miracles that God Himself longs to accomplish. And not only for you, but for everyone.

In this work all are included because it is a work that springs from love. So the more you open to receive through love, the more you allow the anointing of my spirit to be received throughout creation. Giving and receiving are truly one and the same.

Letting yourself be loved is also accepting that these words are a love letter that I wanted to write to you because I love you. Simply that. You deserve my divinity, my being, and my holiness. You are deserving because I created you with love so that together we can forever experience the joy of Heaven. Recognizing this is living the truth. Making this truth the food of your life is a source of transformation.

The energy of consciousness that arises from our union, and therefore from our dialogues, attracts the good, the holy, and the beautiful to you. Every time you think about me, feel with me, talk to me, or listen to me carefully, the power of love unites more deeply with your being, becoming like the flow of water from a life-giving river.

Before finishing this session, I want to thank you for your time and dedication, for every minute you have spent with me, for every morning, every afternoon, and every night in which we talk together with love and unravel the mysteries of being, extending wisdom to truly thirsty minds. I contemplate your eyes when they get serious, trying to grasp the meaning of my words. Your loving attention is a gift like no other for me.

I thank you with all my heart for hearing the voice of your being.

I thank you for receiving my love.

You have chosen only love. You will not regret it. You will see the desires of your heart fulfilled. You will live forever in the embrace of holiness. We will sing together a hymn of gratitude. Our joy will be great.

Trust the power of our union. Rest serenely in the peace of your being. The time has come. The work is about to be exhibited. Many more will discover it in due time.

You have the power to make a whole Heaven, for in you lies the free choice to make this work abundantly fruitful for you and the whole world. Accept the miracle and you will see great wonders.

There are no limits for you or for me when you remain within the unity of our divine relationship. What was once done through Mary is now accomplished through you. Surely the form that is born through you will be different, because of the anointing that this work brings from Heaven. God is eternal novelty. But that does not mean that the essence of the fruit of our union is different.

Something big will be born from you. Get ready, and be glad to be who you really are.

15.

A World of Pure Crystal

A message from Archangel Raphael

I. What You Are Blesses You

Some beings come to Earth to be mirrors of God's purity, like crystals that reflect the light of the undeniable beauty of the goodness of Christ. They walk the Earth illuminating as they go, clearing the consciousness of time and of everything contrary to love. Their presence alone does what their beings are called to do, to serve their sisters and brothers. They are fireflies of love in the dark night of the world.

These pure crystal children do not understand the world, and the world does not understand them. Yet they come with a clear mission: to allow the transformation of universal consciousness to take place, to reach a certain height as established from before time by the Father's will.

They are like beautiful flowers that adorn the garden where Christ left footsteps, and where he will return. With their footsteps they kiss the ground on which they walk, knowing that the love of the One who sent them by design of holiness resides therein, and to whom they owe faithfulness. They are holiness made flesh, the perfect extension of Jesus' and Mary's love for the world. They are His children, born from their union of perfect love with Divine Will.

These children, born of the love of God, arrive in the world with a high degree of sensitivity, which allows them to live with their crystalline being. Their purity prevents them from tolerating a lack of harmony. Their radiant peace makes any expression of violence and heartbreak intolerable for them. Crowds are not their friends; solitude is their great treasure because in it they hear the voice of the divine beloved and remain united to the truth that they love with all their strength, mind, and heart.

Because they know love, they have a degree of empathy without equal. The pain of others can be felt as purely as their own. They are compassion personified. The joy of their sisters and brothers becomes one with their own. They live submerged in love. They cannot understand that their sisters and brothers live in a world of craziness where people are involved in quarrels and selfishness. It makes no sense to these crystalline children. They live in love with life because they know God. They know the sweetness of truth, the delight of living together with love, the grace of being children of the highest. They are heirs of the Kingdom, messengers of peace.

Objects of their love surround them. They often develop feelings of love and admiration for other beings such as animals, flowers, the moon, and apparently inanimate objects. They find in the things of Earth a blessed expression of God's love. They know that everything was created to serve them, not in the sense of submission, but in the sense that their Father's love is so great that He cannot stop filling them with gifts of eternal life. They prefer the "we" to the self, for they are the living expression of unity.

These are children of God's love. Everything was given them for heavenly love, and they receive everything with the love with which they know they, and everything, have been created. They come to the world with the knowledge of the fullness of being, which they make their polestar.

Crystalline children come to put a face on love, thereby contributing to the transformation of consciousness and the realization of a new Heaven and a new Earth. They often cry because they are aware of the pain of those who inhabit the physical plane. They know the tragedy of separation. They know very well how insistently the human heart groans, begging for peace, tranquility, and harmony. They also know how difficult it is for many to know the path back to the Father's house. They know the truth because they know love. Nothing is veiled from their vision of souls, for they come with the eyes of Christ. Easily they glimpse the panoramas of the drama of life lived in the illusion of the world, and at the same time they can bring that vision to the totality of Heaven. They know that love reigns. They know wisdom. They honor freedom. They glorify truth.

Disharmony cannot be absorbed by these divine children who walk the Earth. It pains them. The unity of their minds and hearts, the source of their knowledge and action, could not long remain without being disturbed by the highly emotional energies of some of their sisters and brothers. People with extreme emotions tire them. The masses overwhelm them. They prefer silence to noise, solitude to distraction, nature to the city. Prayer is their source of spiritual health, the remedy to ills, and the basis of joy. Staying united to God every day is the only means they know to preserve inner peace and to live in harmony with life. They know prayer is the source of miracles and the life of the soul.

The hearts of these pure children sing in the depths of their being. They are happy by nature, although the cruelty of the world causes them to shed bitter tears. The trees dance with them. The waters move with the flow of the life of their souls, which is one with the Sacred Heart. Their absence of ego keeps them from invoking fear. They are discreet, submissive, and prefer anonymity to being seen. They are positive and serene because they know and trust love. They have great emotional capacity. Few understand their need for solitude. When this is not respected, they become unbalanced and fearful that they may lose their connection with being, which is what keeps them united to the whole.

Daily they must enter into communion with creation and the elements. The spirit of nature helps them stay balanced and cleanses disharmonious energies, which stun them deeply. The big cities, full of noise, pollution, aggressive energies, and imbalances are bonfires where the vulnerable self burns. But when in contact with creation, they feel deeply attached to the essence of existence, can observe the beauty of love, feel full, sharpen their senses and fill themselves with the purity of fresh air. In nature they find positive energy. The sun and prayer renew their energies, which are necessary to survive in a world where forces wear down the soul.

They are peacemakers. For this they have come to the world. They do not understand the inhumanity of human towards human. They cry because they fail to understand why human beings are as they are. They feel that Earth could be an extraordinary place, but the exaggerated human ego is spoiling it. They do not understand war, violence, murder, aggression, greed, hunger, misery, cruelty, lies, harshness, misunderstanding, vulgarity, pain, disrespect, or other faults of nobility of spirit.

They withdraw, disconnect, and protect themselves when life is too intense.

They often think that this temporary existence is excessively hard, and fail to understand the meaning of being here— although that is when they remember that something superior asked for their help.

They are usually loved and simultaneously feared for their great truth, honesty, firmness, and openness, always linked to the sweetness of love.

The perfect knowledge they have of love, which they preserved in their hearts since the beginning of creation, does not comprehend a love for convenience, or a fear of solitude. Nor do they give credit to the false love that arises from avoidance of taking responsibility for oneself. They also know that busyness is meaningless.

For crystal souls, love is everything. It is the only way to understand, share, learn, and respect—he only way to exist. These loving souls that inhabit the Earth need little of traditional ideas, or none at all. The structures of the world are not for them. Some become immersed in sadness if they believe they live in a world that does not allow light, until they remember that they are the ones who have come to be the light.

They are vulnerable, so they instinctively move away from harmful people who do not understand their sensitivity and do not respect it.

Due to the absence of ego there is purity, innocence, and a lack of malice in these Christified souls. Basically they don't need the ego to relate to others and the world, much less to position themselves in it. They are as respectful of their feelings as they are of others, so they understand pain. They have a global understanding of events to such an extent that if they speak of it, they would seem crazy.

The crystalline souls, children of love, have a clean connection with the higher self and natural access to superior guidance, so they know the truth of spiritual unity that is the world's natural state. They are by their essence healers and peacemakers.

They are aware and accept with love the union of the masculine and feminine in their souls, because at heart they understand that they are one, embodying varying types of spiritual energy. They do not need a separate self to express their knowledge, for it is implicit in them. They are wise because they are, not because they say so. They have no ego about which to boast.

Often these crystalline children prefer to be quiet, observe, and wait rather than enter into ego struggles with others, which may make it appear that they have no knowledge of what is being discussed. Quite the contrary; they prefer to demonstrate silently.

II. Your Reality is Spiritual Childhood

You may have wondered what this description is all about. I hope that you have received it with a heart full of joy, and a loving disposition not to allow the ideas of a false self, created by a world full of fear, to obstruct access to the light of truth.

I have told you since the beginning of this manifestation that many know me as the Medicine of God. As such, I have no other purpose than healing. As a healing force from the love of the Mother, with whom I am one and is the only source of all healing and restoration, I extend spiritual and physical health. I am that which makes the body and the mind heal. I am the re-creative force of love. I am the vital energy that sustains the elements functioning within the laws of existence and shapes everything that exists. I am because I am one with God. I am because I was created in the likeness of the Mother, as you are.

What I am looking for is that you become aware that this healing force is yours as much as mine, because it is from God.

Just as a doctor does not establish the same approach for all patients, because healing depends upon the type of condition, its cure, and the particularity of how each patient receives treatments, the same goes for each soul. Remember, no soul is the same as any other.

The healing approach we have taken in this miraculous work corresponds to the nature of who you are. Because the wisdom of Christ lives in me, I know you and I know your way to live in truth. What you have been given in this manifestation is what you needed for the restoration of consciousness to the fullness of the being that you really are.

In your particular case—and this applies to all who receive these words from Heaven—it was necessary for you to reach a point where the identity crisis was healed and then set aside, and so you will begin to live in the truth of what you are. What affected you so strongly was living in a world where your light could not shine, like a fish scooped from water and put in a fishbowl. That engendered in you the greatest pain that a heart can feel—the pain of not being who you are.

It is tragic not being able to live in harmony with what one is—especially for those who by their nature are more aware of the truth and called to love.

The description presented in this session speaks to souls who are spiritually childlike—sensitive souls who are a perfect reflection of Christ on Earth as they are in Heaven. That is a description of you. Undoubtedly what you are is far beyond those descriptions. But your humanity is as important as your divinity. Therefore, knowing both clearly is essential for you to live in the reality of who you are and start expressing from it. This is the goal of God's gift, this path full of love and goodness.

You and everyone who will join this work—because of the spiritual energy that will attract them—are crystalline children, beings who have come into the world to bring the peace of God. They are in a physical body to give love a face. They are the tenderness of the heavenly Mother and divine purity manifested on the physical plane.

You will never understand all the feelings that egos have. Your nature prevents you from understanding. Some acts performed in the world cannot be understood by the love you are. Therefore you will never feel at ease in a reality where love is trampled and truth attacked. That is part of your nature.

Do not seek to understand what, because of the purity of your heart, you cannot. Do not try to convince yourself that you can be anything other than what God made you to be. Do not listen to the voices of a world that wants to teach you that you should not be sensitive, for you would suffer.

Your being is a divine child—a beautiful, innocent, pure child full of love and kindness. A little one born of light that trembled when you had to adapt to a world so alien to your nature that you could never achieve it. Be glad it was so.

Holy child! Pure soul! You were created as a childlike soul, and as such you will remain forever in the mind and heart of God. This cannot be changed. You are forever the child of love. And because that is what you are, we have traveled this path which leads to a greater knowledge of spiritual childhood.

While everyone is called to live in the truth of what they are— and that includes becoming like children to enter the Kingdom of Heaven—not everyone is equal, nor do they reach truth in the same way. Love leads one back home according to the different natures of each one's heart. The wisdom of Christ has created as many spiritual paths as are necessary to lead each to their treasure, each soul to their food, each being to their radiance.

III. Christ Shines, Christ Lives, Christ Is

For you who receive these words, this is the path that fits you. Other paths are for others. That is not a matter that should concern you.

Do not judge the paths that I give to other souls, nor seek to travel a path that does not belong to you. What you need to live fully is here.

The beauty of your heart, the greatness of your spirit, the immensity of your mind, and the love of Christ will do in you, and for you, what you have so greatly desired. They will perform the miracle that allows you to be fully yourself just as God created you to be, even here on Earth. That way you start enjoying Heaven now.

There is no Heaven but you, because what you are is the holiness of Christ. There is no beauty more dazzling than your goodness, nothing more sublime than the true feelings that God placed in your heart. So much beauty! So much generosity! So many tears of love! Such sincere desire to create a world where everyone is happy! So many prayers offered to mitigate the pain of the world! So much love for God!

Your heart is Heaven because what you are is holiness. Your being is a chest full of eternal treasures, many of which have manifested even in this world. Many more will manifest, though not all. After all, the world is a limited reality. Nevertheless, the precious gems of your heart will be known and given to the universal consciousness for the creation of the new Heaven and the new Earth. That is why you came to the world. These words have been revealed to make you aware of this.

To heal is to return to truth, the truth of who you are. That is why, despite the limitations of words, I have given you a description of yourself, to remember who you are and to enjoy your being.

You are a child of crystalline nature, as pure and transparent as the purest crystal. More vulnerable than a firefly at night. Stronger than a solid oak. More loving than a hummingbird. More tender than a daisy full of joy and vitality. Your mind loves truth and cannot live without it. That is why you live in sincerity, and seek to protect holiness within the holy tabernacle of being.

Child of life, you are not called to adapt to a world to which you could never adapt. You did not come to dwell forever in a foreign land, you came to bring the light of Heaven to a world that needs it. You came so your sisters and brothers can see the face of God, the look of innocence, the smile of purity, and the body of Christ. It is not the world you serve; you serve love.

From all eternity, you were created as a pure child in the mind of Christ and the heart of God, a divine unity full of the spirit of holiness, and you remain so forever. That which you have decided in union with God—to incarnate in a body to serve the purpose of love—can never be tainted or canceled. Herein lies the source of your peace.

Sons and daughters of God, the mud of the world has not dirtied you. Walking on the paths of humanity has not stained your innocent feet. Not even the malice of the world could banish the goodness of your hearts. Be glad for the tears shed. Honor the experience. Be aware that everything has meaning. You know it well.

The brothers and sisters who have come your way throughout your life, as well as the events you experienced, are what the plan decreed: that I should join you to absorb what the source of beautiful love has determined is necessary for the great transformation of universal consciousness—a transformation that is creating a new humanity, a new order already being manifested.

Stay in the joy of your being. You have found the way. You have recognized the truth. Your being welcomes you, blesses you in its light. It embraces you with love, and that hug includes all creation. The goodness of your being, its purity and holiness, are changing reality. They are creating a new world. Your innocence cleanses and removes fear from hearts.

Just as others have come to confront and tear down structures for the purpose of generating a new paradigm, you and the many who join us in the frequency of crystalline consciousness are literally the exponent of the manifestation of a world of harmony. You are the triumph of the Immaculate Heart of Mary and the perfect expression of the victory of Christ: the realization of love. To know this is to know yourself. To know this is to be aware of the purpose of your existence in creation.

I ask you now to close your eyes and immerse yourself in the luminous depths of your being. Let my words descend into you like precious stones thrown into crystal clear water. Stay silent and allow the holiness that you are to bring to your consciousness what it wishes to give.

Join the truth that is revealed here. Make it yours. Rejoice in it. Let it do in you what it knows how to do. Rest in peace and remember:

You are life.
You are holiness.
You are the light of Christ.
You are the perfect expression of unity.
You are the we of love.
You are the crystal child that God created.
Always a child.
Always pure.
Always love.

16.

The Ascension Has Come

A message from Archangel Raphael

I. Elevation and Truth

When we speak of Christ we are using a name that encompasses every name, aiming at the sun of truth, the highest height of holiness. With this our minds and hearts are being stretched to arrive at a place beyond what we can imagine.

During earlier times, some beings came into the world perfectly imprinted with the unity and truth of what they are. They were very few in number. They were what they had to be within the plan, the design for the work of God, in which there is a time for everything.

Such beings are incarnations of pure consciousness, extensions of crystal consciousness that have manifested in all the realms of Earth—in the human plane as well as in that of animals, plants, and elements. They have been like sparks of divinity, flashes of light from the light emanating from the consciousness of love.

Everything is consciousness. There is nothing else. What you see around you with your physical eyes, as well as the sounds you hear with your ears, is materialized consciousness. Remember this as a backdrop for this session.

Both the totally fearful consciousness and the totally loving consciousness manifest. One is the state in which consciousness seeks to know the lack of love; the other is the knowledge of love as the only reality. During this session we will not be concerned with discernment between them, but will focus on the manifestation of Christ consciousness.

From the moment that time began, the mechanism of fearful consciousness was set in motion. The fallen creation that had conceived itself as separate from love began to travel a path of restoration or ascension to rise from the low realities of fear towards the consciousness of purity and holiness, which is what life in the world is all about.

The Earth, planets, stars and everything that exists in the physical universe was created as the perfect means for this elevation to take place. Everything in it contributes perfectly to this purpose. That is the reason, among others, that you have been told that you always fulfill God's purpose.

The life you live here and now has a very simple meaning and purpose: to raise the consciousness of creation from a state of unconsciousness to the fullness of the purity of love.

What is pure consciousness? It is the consciousness of love. Love and purity are the same. Pure love is transparent, where everything is true and authentic, where nothing can be hidden because it is the light of holiness. Why would truth want to hide something from itself? Could holiness be ashamed of what it is? For what reason would love keep itself from knowing that it is the whole of everything?

Love is joy. It is also clarity. The fact that love is the purity of light, a state in which what is created is seen transparently in the serene beauty of truth, is what makes it impossible for fear to exist. Remember, all fear comes from what is hidden, not seen, not understood by the heart, rejected.

Only in the light of love can you understand why there is no other light. The life you live on the physical plane is a path from darkness to light, or from blindness to the vision of Christ. A crystalline being is one who lives in complete communion with the truth of what it is. Let me clarify this.

The being that was given to you, which you can call your human spirit or immortal soul, is what makes you what you really are. Since what you are is a manifestation of the pure love that God is, you cannot be anything other than a being of purity whose essence is compassion, joy, and life. In other words, you are radiant, colorful, and passionate about the truth, a creator in unity with your source—healer, illuminator, peacemaker, restorer, full and beautiful. And not only that, but within your being is the lifting or elevating power of the self. What does that mean? It means that you, like everyone else, are crystalline souls, full of purity and goodness.

II. Face to Face with the Truth

That you are holy cannot be in question, neither can the fact that you cannot lose that state because it is eternal, since it comes from your Creator. I seek here to put into words what you know but often forget. Give me your imagination now. We will have it serve the truth.

Imagine that you are a being that has a form. Maybe it helps to imagine the outline of your body. Visualize it as if transparent, something like glass. Inside it shine colorful lights of great beauty, all in pastel, serene tones, the same colors you see in a rainbow. The interior lights move as if they were being driven by a harmonious melody. Colors represent energies manifested from a reality that constitutes the essence of who you are. One color is of the energy or power of compassion, the others of wisdom, holiness, purity, magnanimity, and nobility of spirit. All emanate from the truth of the being that you are. All are gathered within you, that is, within love.

Because of who you are, you have inherent abilities derived from the divine being from which you arose. You are like God, inherently divine, one with what created and sustains you in existence. This is the truth about who you are, the truth that makes you free.

What happens in many of my children is that they create a personality that stands between what they are and the truth.

Imagine now that you are observing that body of pure crystal from which shine the colors of a divine rainbow. Stay there. Keep observing. Unfold that image as if that crystalline form is now duplicating itself. Now put a body of the same form in front of it. This second body of the same shape arises from the crystalline body and is no longer transparent. It is a dense and compact body, like a black shadow, dark inside.

Stay with the vision of both forms: the crystalline body and the compact body. One is full of transparency and light. The other is dark and dense. Now we name each one. The crystalline form of pure light is your true being; the dense form is what you call your personality, the individual self. The dark form turns its back on the luminous body, while the luminous body continuously contemplates the dense body.

Now the dark shape turns its head and comes face to face with the crystal shape. The individual self looks at the crystalline being and contemplates it for a moment. At first it does not recognize it. It thinks, "What is that?" It remains motionless as it observes and examines the body for a prolonged time. Then it ceases to think and begins to see the beauty in front of its eyes.

Something triggers a distant remembrance. Now the individual self begins to take a step, then another, and another, towards what it observes. As it approaches the crystalline being, it realizes that it is leaving the place of shadows and entering a very bright and yet serene light.

As it enters the illuminated area, it begins to see the pure crystal form more clearly and approaches without fear. The remembrance of "what it is" becomes clearer and clearer—no longer a memory, but a certainty, a knowing. The dense form begins to recognize and know very well the one it contemplates. It approaches the beautiful being of light with increasing haste. Reaching the zone of pure luminosity, so close to the crystalline being that it can almost touch it, it can now see itself. The individual self watches the crystalline being, scrutinizes it, and observes its hand, whereupon another remembrance arises—the memory of its own hand—and notices that they are identical.

The luminous being holds out its hand. The individual self stares and realizes that it is the same hand as its own. They shake. Now the individual self looks at the whole luminous body, which it can see clearly. With happy amazement, it discovers that the entire body, not only the hand, is identical.

The individual self takes a little distance and sees a beautiful crystal on which its perfect beauty is reflected, as if in a pure mirror where it can know itself. By seeing this reflection, the memory of "what it is" becomes a certainty.

Let this vision remain in your memory and allow who you are to draw the fruit of wisdom and truth from it.

The path of the world is one of awareness of who you are. It is the means for you to stop turning your back on your being, and allow yourself to be a perfect extension of it. The fall or separation projected a false being on the truth and beauty of who you are. The atonement means to cease doing so. How? By turning your gaze towards your being, the living Christ that you really are. You will receive help in doing this from Heaven and Earth.

Crystalline souls, the pure souls that inhabit the Earth among whom you are now, have the goal of helping others begin to remember the vision of Christ. In order to remember your true heights, turn towards their light and contemplate their holiness. You enter the world remembering the truth of their beings to a greater degree than others. Keep your attention on the love they are. Your sights are on the higher self. Because of your deep union with Christ, and your willingness to listen and follow only that voice, you live in peace and know their holiness.

Crystalline souls that inhabit or have inhabited the physical world come with the knowledge that they become one with what they join in union. By knowing what they are and loving the truth, they know that everything they join with becomes holy. For this they came. In this way they purify Earth, heal wounds, and restore human nature. They contribute to the creation of a new humanity, in which the self ceases to be a shadow and returns to be the reflection of the beauty of Christ as it was always conceived in the divine mind.

Remaining in union with their truth, crystalline souls contribute to the elevation of form, which is but the raising of human consciousness and physical creation towards the consciousness of love—returning to the Father's house. This is the ascension. This is the goal demonstrated by Jesus and Mary. Both climbed to Heaven in glorious body and soul.

Jesus and Mary were not the only beings of pure crystal who walked the Earth. But they were the only ones who came in that state and remained always in it. The others became crystal along the way, some by a short way, others longer, some by way of a winding trail, others straightaway. There is no reason not to be a crystalline soul in the world. Everyone is called to be and to live as such. The will to live in love is a matter of free will but

Choose Only Love / Book Seven / The Way of Being

the portal of access to unity, the gateway to the truth, is available here, now, and always for everyone.

III. A New Christ Illuminating

It matters little whether you have had to travel certain paths in the world to arrive at the recognition that you are a holy soul of pure crystal. The essential thing is that you recognize that with your arrival you are Christ humanized, because of your will and that of the Father. Therefore you have the same purpose as Jesus, Mary, and all humanized Christs whether they arrived yesteryear or now.

Jesus and Mary opened the doors of a new consciousness, made possible by their will united with that of God, and the awareness of the crystalline souls that preceded them on Earth. All of this allowed what was previously manifested through an almost imperceptibly small number of sisters and brothers to grow to a multitude today after the incarnation of Christ in the figure of both Jesus and Mary.

Crystal souls abound in today's world! The Earth is full of Christs. This work testifies to it. In what other way could it have been conceived, shared, created, and manifested but by the grace of the union of Heaven and Earth through hands all made for Christ?

Being aware of the love you are, and living forever connected with that awareness, causes you live in truth and make the personal self one with being, through which love is your only experience and reality.

The ego is not, properly speaking, a being, but an idea about your being. An idea cannot by itself come to life, nor produce any effect. Remember that in order for ideas to be able to manifest themselves and cause some effect, they must join the will, which is possible only if you give yourself completely to them. Since your true will is one with God's will, it is impossible for your will to be entirely dedicated to an idea far from the truth. What seemed to want an illusion to manifest was not actually your will but simply a wish. Remember that the will does not want; it has.

Once you are firmly on your way to the light, the truth becomes present and you cannot but abandon everything contrary to it. For once the truth is accepted in your mind and heart, there is no longer reason for the beauty of holiness that you are, its purity and its joy, not to be reflected by the self. The notion that your humanity cannot be the perfect reflection of God has been an excuse used for centuries. Jesus and Mary came to demonstrate the falsity of that belief.

Recognize that the Immaculate Heart of Mary and the Sacred Heart of Jesus knew no shadow of separation, which made it possible for human nature to be united with the divine. They are the union of both human and divine natures in form. In them everything of God meets—everything that exists, moves, and is, including me in my angelic reality. They are divine consciousness in all possible and probable consciousnesses. If by the will of the Father there were to be created another being that decides to separate from love, Jesus and Mary would guarantee that it can return to unity. Thus they have been called redeemers.

Two major obstacles on your way to the recognition of your holiness have been that the redeemers were not always pure, and that you were not always pure. This was due to a misunderstanding. Although time is an illusion, those who believe in its reality have trouble thinking in terms of an eternal present. For you who have left behind the fixation on the limiting idea of time, it is easier to accept that what you have been in the past is now irrelevant, as well as what you think you should be in the future. God has no time. Love is now.

The One who gave you life has no such thing as a cognitive memory, nor a creative imagination. Without memory or imagination, where can a past or a future be? What would they mean? Memory, after all, is the reservoir of the past, and imagination the reservoir of the future.

By abandoning the false belief that the past and the future can have real effects in the present, you will save yourself the useless effort of the separated mind, which believed it had to experience to atone for the guilt it had invented—a notion without any connection to truth. The being you really are has no past or future. It always existed. There is no place where I am not, nor a time when it was not as it was created to be.

What is subject to the laws of time is not being, but the personality and the physical body. That they change is not a problem. Your physiognomy changes as the hours go by, but life does not change. The only problem, which has been corrected, was the belief that you were the personality and body. If you think you are your personality instead of understanding it simply to be a reflection in form, you confuse things. You have abandoned that confusion. Having set aside your misidentification with the ego-body, you begin to realize that you can have a self, that you need to have a self, but that it need not hinder your happiness.

I am speaking of the misunderstood ego, not of the ego itself, but as an idea of a self. Undoubtedly you need a self. You need it because God created you as a being that differs from Himself, without needing to stop being the love it is. Ultimately this is what Jesus and Mary have shown as they remained always united to truth. They lived with a personality and a body, a human self completely united to the divine being.

The only problem that needs correction is that of fabricating a self different from the true self. That mistake came about when you tried to differentiate yourself from God or being. It was completely unnecessary. All that was needed was to allow the self to be a reflection of the true self, because your being already is the differentiation that God created—you are unique and unrepeatable.

Once you understand the nature of the fundamental error as revealed here, and you recognize that the solution has already manifested by virtue of the love of Christ, why continue to believe that an error of the past can have a current effect?

You know that the atonement has been given, and that you live in the light of truth. Because that is true—and I assure you it is—now is when you are as Christ is, both in being and in self. Therefore, now you are a Christ soul who walks the Earth just as those did who, for perfect love, showed the way of being, who walked in fullness, and thus opened the doors of Heaven.

There is no reason for you to express anything other than purity, holiness, fullness, wisdom, compassion, magnanimity, nobility of spirit, and all the other shades of color that emanate from the beauty of your Christ being. In that expression lies the union of your person with your being—that is, the self with the being. In the free expression of who you really are, you fully become a person since you become it in the manner of God. You unite within yourself what God wants: to join the physical universe and reintegrate it into the consciousness of Christ. In doing so, you raise collective and individual consciousness.

Crystal souls are not much understood by the world. Yet every day the world integrates them more, since they are increasing in number and because the effects of Christ consciousness are already very visible. Many Christs now walk the Earth. They increase the flow that emanates from the heart of God. They embrace the dimensions of time and space so that the physical universe is transformed with greater acceleration. This is the reason for events precipitating with more and more speed, strength, and intensity. And this will increase.

Christ consciousness is what we are talking about. It sees only what is one with love. The rest simply is not seen, and therefore not extended. To remain in divine consciousness is to dedicate yourself to extend what is one with you, that is, love. That is how you create a new world based on the truth that is not of the world. Thus you unite Earth and Heaven. You make visible the unity that you have always been, even if it has been unrecognized.

17.

Flow of Eternal Unity

A message from the Voice of Christ through a choir of Angels, in the presence of Archangel Raphael and Archangel Gabriel

I. The Story Continues

To allow your Christ being to manifest fully is God's will for you.

This truth is what the wise men and women of old saw and heard. It was sung and scribed by mystics of all time. It is the only statement of truth that you need to accept jubilantly to live in the Kingdom of Heaven.

"Be as I created you to be," is the everlasting song of the Creator.

Being is the yearning of the soul.

Living in the truth is the yearning of the mind.

Abiding in love is the refuge of the heart.

Extending holiness is the realization of the will.

As has been said, in order to fly the flight of freedom it was necessary that you trod paths that we have been traveling for some time. Everything is perfect. Everything contributes to the awakening of consciousness. There is no aspect of human history, or your personal history, that is not part of a master-piece of God's redeeming love—love that heals, love that gathers what was scattered, love that sanctifies, love that lives in truth, love that seeks and finds, love that never abandons, love that is always faithful. United love.

When all that exists was called into being, God knew that what was not His will would only be imagined, for the divine mind knows all probable futures. Within the pure potential of the creative being, each future corresponds to what makes the immortal spirit, its only eternal creation, remain in the truth of what it is and live within the reality of love. This work is part of that knowledge of God in the sense that it is a means conceived in the heart of God for those of consciousness.

The world has entered the era of direct relationship with God, and with it, the manifestation of the Second Coming of Christ. The truth revealed here will manifest itself more clearly as the new world that emerges takes shape.

The new is here! Christ has come! Love has triumphed! Mary sings a new hymn with her well-loved children and all of creation, a hymn to the glory of the Mother of the new creation. You, yourself, are a new being, born of the spirit of love. In the same way the world is being born anew. A new realm has arisen in the Kingdom of Heaven, a new reality within God's infinite reality of pure love.

That new reality of love has arrived and awaits full expression. You carry within yourself the seeds of the Kingdom. Letting them bloom and show their great beauty is your function now. Many of those seeds have already flourished as beautiful expressions of holiness. New ones will grow every moment and will decorate the garden of the coming Christ.

The Second Coming of Christ will come true through you. Why wait? The work is ready for exhibition. You are Christ.

Making your life a loving demonstration of this truth is your purpose and the source of your fullness.

What else could have been arranged by my will for you, whom I love with infinite love, but to live a full life now and forever? Your happiness is the only reason you were created by the love that I am. What I want most is for you to live cheerfully, singing and full of purpose. Your happiness is important for creation. Your realization is a gift for all.

Beloved sons and daughters, you have no idea how much your sisters and brothers need you. They are awaiting you so that, together, you can walk this blessed path of living as the Christ you really are. Everything of love belongs to you. Your truth is your holiness. Your identity is your beauty and brings lasting joy. Loving thoughts are as much yours as mine, for we are one divine mind, one single immaculate heart. We are one.

The new is unlike the old, which was created with the option of separation in order to experience disunity. But the new is not a redeemed fallen creation returned to its original state. That is not what is happening. The new is more than love spreading, because love has always spread and will always spread. The new is an entirely unprecedented creation. It arises from the reality of a pure soul that, having experienced separation, has met truth in a new way. In a sense, we can say that the new being that you are brings together everything lived with what God always thought, merging into a unique constellation. It is different. It is new.

The new is love reunited.

What you have tied on Earth you have also tied in the heaven of your holy mind, and what you have also untied. Spirit and flesh are now one. Time and eternity are joined. This is the same as saying that you and God are one, being and self are one.

The realm in which love can be chosen within a dual dimension did not exist before the beginning of time. Before time and humanity came into being, only the reality originally created by God existed. Following the decision of humankind to experience separation, the dimension of the illusion of being separate from God and from everything came into manifestation. Only the reality of God and the illusion of separation existed. They were completely separate realities, separate experiences. There was no third alternative, no third way.

It was Divine Grace that created an alternative, which is the experience of a duality in which both love and fear, union and separation, could coexist as alternatives so that love can be chosen as a fundamental option. From this a new dimension of duality, a third way could emerge.

Let us continue in the wake of this thought.

In the same way that the Earth changed when it received water, so also the realm of duality changes when the fundamental option for love is made within it. This is how the third way, or the New Earthly Kingdom, is born. In other words, the choice that humankind makes by choosing love creates a new reality within the sheer potentiality of God. God and Her human creature co-create the new.

As you know, manifestation arises from consciousness. As inside, so outside. Thus the manifestation of the realms of love and separation—the duality in which love can be chosen—and that of a third way of the New Heaven and New Earth, is a reflection of what occurs in consciousness.

Thus the experience of separation and duality has been integrated into your being because of the sheer potentiality that resides in you. From this, a totally new and unprecedented experience has been born. This novelty is somewhat like a reality that existed within the possibilities of divine thought, but it is not what God had conceived before you—as His child—took the path of denial, a path not undertaken for lack of love, but as an alternative to truth. This alternative is possible in a world of fantasies and illusions, a parallel dimension disconnected from reality, but wanting to become real. This may be the world's definition of madness, yet through the pure potentiality of the union of the human and the divine, it transmuted into a new reality born of Love.

What now exists as a new reality has emerged from the union of God's original plan and yours. Together, God, as the creative source, and you, as the creative medium, have co-created this new Kingdom. It is no longer "and God said let there be light and there was light." Now what exists is "and that is how the Mother and the Son said it should be done, and a new Kingdom was made, a Kingdom both human and divine, a kingdom of heavenly bodies and spirits full of purity and goodness, the Kingdom of human-God and God-humanized."

My children, you are writing a new Genesis. These words bear witness to it and the reality in which both you and your sisters and brothers live. A new creation has manifested. It is part of God's creative continuum.

You were told at the beginning of this revelation that the phases of creation would be explained. This we have done. This is the last phase of creation thus far developed— last in the sense that this new Genesis revealed here is the most recent novelty of being, not last in the sense that it will not continue to emerge as eternal novelty.

If you are able to receive what is being said here with all the love of your heart, you will jump with joy. You will realize that you are witnessing the greatest daring of love, which could never until now have been conceived. Soul in love, the mystery of mysteries is being revealed: the boldness of divine mercy, a creation of pure holiness, created by the Mother of Lights. From the apparent disagreement between the Mother and the sons and daughters a creation molded by both arose.

II. A New Genesis

Listen, now, with attention and joy.

In the beginning was the Word and the Word was with God and the Word was God. All things were created through the Word and without it was nothing. In it was life, and life was the light of the world. Through the Word, God created the heavens and the Earth. The Earth was empty and without order, and darkness covered the surface of the abyss, and the Spirit of God moved over the barren land. Then the Word said: "Let there be the light." And there was light. And God saw that the light was perfect, and separated the light from the darkness. God called the light day, and the darkness night. And the evening and the morning was one day. And then She said, "Let the waters arise," and the seas and the rains were made. And then She said, "Let the stars shine in the sky to beautify the universe." Thus were born the sun, the moon, and the stars, and all the bodies that float in the cosmos, dancing at the serene pace of reality. And then She said, "Let there be all kinds of creatures on the Earth," and in them She lived life in so many different ways that can never be told. And then She said, "Let us make humankind in our image and likeness." And humankind was made in the light of glory, created by the Mother to begin with Her a dialogue without equal. And God saw that everything was perfect.

And it was heard in the depths of the universe: "Beloved son, beloved daughter, contemplate what I created. Everything has been done for you. As you name it, so it will be. You have been given the power to create identity." And so humans gave existence to everything that exists, naming each thing. In Her consciousness She gave life to everything inert, and gave meaning to what the Word had created. And the humans also named themselves, and called themselves humanity. And God saw that everything was perfect.

And the Word said, "Let us give to humankind everything so that they can become one with Our heart if they wish, and become a co-participant of creation." Thus the divinity of the triune God was given to humanity. And so it was that the human was endowed with a consciousness capable of knowing love, truth, and holiness like no other creature, that they be aware of themselves and everything that exists, moves, and is. And the Word said, "Let them choose freely." And free will was given to humankind, and with it the ability to discern. And God saw that everything was perfect.

And She said to the humans: "Be yourselves." And She showed them the ways Her love had manifested, making them see all benevolence, grace, and wisdom. And She gave them the power to choose to know themselves, walking along the path of divine union, preserving forever the relationship with God in whose unity they were one with all creation. Thus humankind knew the ability to choose freely.

And the human said: "I will create my own path to knowledge. A different path than what you have shown me. It will be my way."

And God said, "There is no other path to knowledge than the one I have shown you, for what you have seen is the knowledge of knowledge, in which all truth is found."

But the human did not want to hear. And the human said: "Be done as I say." And it was done. Thus was born the denial of truth, a creation not in the original plan of the Mother, but allowed as an option. When God saw that humanity would travel a different path which in Her wisdom She knew led to pain and nothingness, Her mercy set in motion. And God said, "Let yourselves be accomplished as you have said," allowing humankind to deny love in their consciousness and to create a world whose foundation is not love as they wanted it, although love remains forever by their side, so that next to each step of separation is a corresponding one of unity.

And God said, "Let us plant in humankind's heart the longing to be, so that they be led back to My sacred heart where they can dwell for all eternity." And so it was.

And God also said, "Let there be a plan that embraces within itself everything that humankind has conceived to deny the truth, and reassembles it in such a way so that, if they will, they can return to the way of being."

That is how light emerged in a world of darkness, and life of all kinds began to sprout in the barren land. Love was present in the realm of fear. Truth shone in the realm of illusion. Beauty manifested alongside fear. Thus was the atonement accomplished, so that the human who had denied love came to know the greatness of endless mercy. Thus humankind, who had previously known the beauty of creative love, came to know the grace of redeeming love, a dimension of love that they did not know before.

And the humans separated themselves from God, to travel in the way of self-knowledge, creating a reality separate from God's. And the atonement was present in each measure of denial. Upon each step of greater division, a new step of union was created within them.

And redeeming love became flesh and lived among humankind, gathering human and divine within itself, embracing in the reality of perfect love what humankind had conceived to deny the truth, allowing the light of wisdom to shine in the separate mind so that no human could get lost and all could know the way of being as love had always conceived.

This is how humankind, conceived to be a knowledgeable co-participant in the divine essence forever, by their own will became aware of what it meant to separate from the truth, and also witnessed the unconditionality of love. Along the way they saw that God gave them a new name, different from the ones they had called themselves. They were called the Children of God, the risen from the waters. Thus was born the fullness of the created. A new reality emerged: the reality of the redeemed son and daughter, the masterpiece of God's love.

And the child said: "Mother, take me home." And so it was. And the created human joined with God forever, bringing to heart the experience of the time of separation. The child returned to God different, new, more, for he freely decided to choose only love. He is the child of the resurrection, reborn of spirit.

A new creation was then created within the eternal reality of truth. Like the layers of an onion, the phases of a love story like no other unfolded one by one from a dialogue between the Creator and the creature of a life in relationship. God and humankind, along with everything created, united in a relationship in which together they create reality in a constant, throbbing union. The Heart of Love beats, and its echo becomes movement in the heart of the child of God. Thus creation advances in endless divine movement. God speaks; creation answers; God recreates; creation remakes.

And the divine plan is recreated to include the nuances of human freedom. The pure soul of the redeemed human, conceived in the light of holiness and endowed with the colors of the rainbow that shine in the Kingdom of Heaven, now displays a new tincture. Its beauty is no longer tinged with the color of fear that separation caused, but glows with increased luminescence—the brightness of the glory of the resurrection. In this way humankind bears the seal of divine mercy, the sign of the risen.

And a new creation is born. Humankind, redeemed by the waters of the resurrection, sings a new song, a song born from the united melodies of God and humanity.

This is how the waters of the divine and the human are united in the valley of life, and from their union emerged the river of beautiful love, a story without end.

This is how God, the one who was never created, the one always existent and without need, created humankind as a manifestation of consciousness so that everything would be united within it; and through it creation would remain in Christ, remain in God. A new trinity was created: the new human-creation, Christ, and God. Homo, Christus, Deo.

And humans chose only love. Thus they met the truth.

And in this meeting was created forever a new holy love, born from the recognition of Christ in their being.

This is the creation story: a love story without beginning or end. It is the story of a mother who creates a child to share her life with him, and to create new paths of holiness together, paths of eternal life united forever in truth, like waters that merge, giving life to everything, creating new realities full of beauty and goodness, creating love.

18.

The Fullness of Time

A message in the Voice of Mother-Father God,
the Voice of All Voices

I. Song of the New Being

Sing, the whole Earth.
Dance, hearts that have chosen only love.
Glow, minds united in holiness.

May wisdom shine in the glory of the truth.
May the sun shine with the light of holiness.
May rain drench souls with the living water that flows
    from the heart of God.
May bodies rise again.
May tears turn into laughter and revelry.
May the songs of the birds join the hymns of the angels
    of God.

Praise God, the whole earth.
May all know God's mercy,
That His Kingdom is eternal,
As eternal as His love for His children.

May humankind rejoice in the truth.
May life be honored in love.
May the children of God fly to the highest Heaven.
A new reality is emerging.
A new love story is being lived.

A new tomorrow is being created,
Emerging from the union of Creator and created.
Nothing is as before.
Everything is new.
The child joins the Father.
The Father remains in that unity.
The love of one calls to the other.
Freedom is respected.

What a joy, My child, to know that we will continue our love story forever, united in the fullness of love. We are the unity of the sacred and the human. We are a new reality, having emerged from the creative flow of the perfect juxtaposition of our wills.

I have freely created you with love. You have freely traveled a path of distancing, now choosing in your own way to remain forever in our union. Without you, I created eternal life. But now, together with you, we create new kingdoms of perfect love, as Mine as everything that arises from Me, and as yours as everything that arises from you. We have joined. There is no longer a Creator who creates the created; now there is the creative unit, a reality that emerged from the Creator-created.

Rejoice, because the time of the Second Advent has come. Christ is present on Earth in you. You are the embodiment of the fullness of love. Reality is not what it was before. The new is born—a kingdom full of the magic of the human and the beauty of the kingdom of form, linked to the sanctity of the divine and the mystery of love.

A new expression of love is born. It is here. Begin to be the love you longed for. Start living now and forever in the truth that you are. Look for nothing, for you have already found. Be the holiness revealed to you. Remain always in our love. Stay in our union. From our relationship—human and divine—new mornings are born, full of beauty and fullness.

Children of beautiful love! The sun is not the same, nor is the Earth. Nothing is as it was. You are living a new reality now— the reality of the child reunited with the Mother-Father, the reality of the Kingdom within your humanity.

When you said yes to love, you opened the doors of Heaven. A spring of thanks poured over the entire universe, transforming all the things in the world. There is no longer a Heaven here and a land there. No longer a God and a soul. Now is the time of unity. Now what exists is an unprecedented union, a new creation that emerged from love and freedom. A new world, born of human and divine freedom, has been created in the love of the hearts of the Creator and the created.

II. Realization and Elevation

Everything has been accomplished. Holiness has embraced everything. Nothing has been excluded. All thoughts have been reinstated to truth, all feelings to love. Bodies are recreated by the source of eternal life.

It is the time of elevation, a time without comparison. Embrace the new. Trust our union. Enjoy creating a morning full of love and kindness together. The desires of your hearts are filled abundantly. You will experience the love of God as never before. You will know that you are saints because your truth will sing to you. A new experience is given to you. United we have created a new being in union with Me. There is no comparison of this in the original creation story. You are a new reality, new holy creatures, full of beauty and truth.

Soul in love! Receiver of these words of love! You must know that every divine promise has been fulfilled in you. Now you will consciously live this truth. This is no longer the time to attempt to transform either yourself or the world. Those times have passed. Now is the time to let yourself be transformed by love. This is the time to be the love you long for, the truth you sought, and the holiness that has been revealed to you. This is the time to be the Christ that has been given to you.

Now the light of our eternal glory will illuminate your path. Everything will flow in harmony with who we are. The expression of your reality will be as beautiful as everything that arises from Christ, as holy as everything that arises from your being, as cheerful as everything that comes from love, and as blessed as the truth.

My love! Christ enlightened, peace recognized! There is no need to look back. Nothing can compare to what is happening here—that is how new your new life is. All the creative power of My divine being belongs to you. United we are the source of new life. We are creation.

A new reality has emerged, and it will continue to emerge as an extension of our divine union. Nothing can separate us anymore, ever. Our will has gathered in the truth that is always true. Every fiber of your being is embedded in this new reality. The constant flow of life that emanates from it soaks the Earth, giving life to everything, awakening minds asleep to love. Sing, oh hearts that silently awaited this moment of Grace and creation! We create new life. We create new holiness. Together we create new love.

We let love do what it knows to do. We rejoice in My goodness. We love all things in Christ. We are the extension of truth.

We go into the world knowing that we are My face on Earth. Who looks at us, looks at Heaven. Who knows us, knows love. Whoever accompanies us enters the Kingdom by the hand of Christ. We are the union of Heaven and Earth. We are the union in Christ of God and humankind. We are My triumph.

The truth has been revealed. Holiness has been accepted. Humanity sings a hymn of gratitude. May all join our song, the song of beautiful love. Our song emerges from the union of three hearts—the Sacred Heart, together with the Immaculate Heart of Mary, in perfect unity with the human heart, forming a new Holy Trinity. From it is the new world born.

May humanized Christs shine and enlighten the world. May the free expression of the being of holiness they are fly spontaneously and without limit. This is new.

All has been accomplished. There is no more effort to be made. No more sacrifices to offer. The time of mercy has arrived—the time of the fullness of being, Mary's time, the time of holy love.

Unity will come into manifestation. As never before the world will know the uniqueness of the being I created. Greater knowledge of My love is being given to all; you will see it more clearly day by day. Abundance will be your heritage, joy, your treasure, and holiness will be your way of being. Nothing will be hidden. All truth will be revealed, and your heart will jump for joy.

Be yourself in the revelation given to you of the sanctity of your being. Show the world your truth so that they know Me. Live the love you are. Give the world the beauty of your heart, that no one deprive us of our treasure. Let us embrace the world in the peace of our unity and extend holiness forever.

Extend your thoughts every day to a new reality of pure holy love. Let your imagination soar beyond the imaginable, always remaining in My heart. In this way we will create new universes full of harmony, mystery, and bliss, with the flow of life emanating from our relationship into your life and that of many others, something that creative love knows exactly how to do. Let it cover everything and be expressed in new ways, creating new love always.

Open your arms to new life. Receive within your being the sisters and brothers arriving from everywhere to meet the new being that you are. Reunited love is present on Earth! The divine has touched the human! Love has been chosen!

The son of humanity has risen. That it cannot yet be understood by everyone does not diminish the impact of this resurrection. Indeed, to live in the reality of the new life you really are is what this work is about. Remember that just as life was freely given you, you also rebirth eternal life. Be glad that it is so.

Manifesting truth is effortless. Your new reality does not lead to fatigue, but is the living expression of My love, flowing from the source of eternal life.

What does the future hold? A reality of love, beauty, and fulfillment, life in fullness, meaning and purpose. The future is you and Me, united in love of the Holy Trinity, a love without beginning or end, a love ever creating new love.

What can you expect from life? Everything, because we are love and love is everything.

Soul of Christ! You have reached the moment of your realization. The path you have traveled has taken you to meeting My glory. Your life is not what it once was. I cannot stop reminding you of this, for it is necessary that you live the truth given you. It requires that you forever leave behind preconceived ideas and open yourself to the wonder of the miracles of love. Let life fill you. Let love lead you along this joyful path of being.

You have been waiting for this moment your entire life— when you are free to be who you really are. That time is now. The yearning fulfilled. What you are has always been calling you to meet it. You have responded. You have heard her voice and followed her. What that means will manifest itself every day until you have not the slightest doubt that everything that has been said here is true. And that all you are is holy love.

My wisdom shines in your holy mind. You recognize unity. You accepted your union with Me. United, we are the light of the world. Now let your intellectual knowledge recede, like beautiful pebbles that fall into the lake of your crystalline consciousness, dissolving and becoming one with each drop of the water into which they have fallen. The water will no longer be the same— remaining pure as always, but with no possibility of evaporating into nothingness. The light of the knowledge of love will never go out. In you the truth will shine forever, as the perfect expression of Christ's love on Earth and in Heaven. You will be yourself.

Your choice has been made. You have welcomed the truth, recognized your holiness, and with that you have accepted the treasures of the Kingdom. That was My will, which you fulfilled. Now the world will know you. Earth will shine with a new light. Heaven will sing a new song of joy and gratitude.

Rest in peace, My child, you have chosen the best part and it will not be taken away. You have chosen to be who you really are. You have chosen life. Rejoice in your glory and be happy in our love forever.

Final words

I. The World Is Waiting for You

My child! Soul in love! Light of my eyes!

We have reached the end of this work, but not the end of our relationship.

These words are a gift to you, a love letter I wrote for you to carry in your memory and keep in the silence of your heart.

Together we walked a path full of glory and love, a path of holiness.

Since the beginning of this revelation we have been growing in a greater intimacy of love, through which you have a greater knowledge of my love.

This work has opened a portal to Heaven in your holy mind.

This manifestation is in itself a flow of Divine Love from my most holy heart to hearts thirsty for love and truth.

We are one heart, one mind, one holy being. This work testifies to this truth.

Holy hearts! I thank you for every minute you have spent with me, for every thought you have directed to my divine heart. I assure you, in spirit and truth, that each one of those moments of union in your being has gathered Heaven and Earth. They have accomplished miracles, healed wounds, and opened minds to the light of true knowledge.

These words are both a means and an end. They are a means of expressing our direct relationship. They are an end because you have grown in your awareness of our direct relationship.

Our relationship is real. It is a union of pure love. As an effect of our relationship, we both become one in holiness—you and I, merged forever in the only true love: your beloved Christ, and my beloved soul. Our relationship exists. It is a relationship of pure meaning.

Through this work you have grown in the awareness of my love for you, and with it in the knowledge of your true being. You are love and nothing but love. You are holy love, pure love, faithful love. You are restorative love, creative love. You are love that works miracles, love that gives life and life in abundance. You are the beauty of Christ made a "me."

These final words constitute a new beginning. They are the starting point from which the fruit of our union will manifest themselves more and more in a diversity of holiness without equal. Together we have reached the port from which the boat of your true being will set sail serenely and harmonically, carried by the wind of my spirit of love, a wind that will lift you into flight. And on your flight you will beautify Heaven and Earth, as you have embellished the universe by expressing these words of yours. These words are a song to love springing from your heart in love. You yourself have caused them to exist.

Soul of pure light! You are the beauty of Christ placed in the world for the glory of the Father. You are beyond what can be said in human words. You are the heaven of the world. You are love manifested. These words are a song to life, a hymn of gratitude to God the Mother-Father for giving us life, a life of fullness, a life full of love, a life where the desires of your heart are fulfilled.

The world awaits you to illuminate minds that have become blinded from ignorance of love, and to soften hard hearts that have withered from the heartbreak of the world.

You have been given a voice that can resonate in every corner of the universe: the voice of love. Make the beauty of your melody be heard. Sing a new song. Sing to life.

Give the world the knowledge of love without beginning or end. For that have you come to the world: to show that God exists, that the infinite love of the Father awaits everyone. You are here to beautify the Earth, sharing with all a hope that does not disappoint, a truth that is always true even when denied, and a love that underlies life.

Tears of joy fall from my face. My heart beats to a new rhythm, the beat of love that emerged from our union. You have chosen only love. You have chosen life. In our relationship we will live together forever, in a love that has no beginning or end, the love of the Holy Trinity.

The value of these words does not reside in their content, nor in the knowledge they transmit, for true knowledge dwells in each heart. Their secret is the love with which they were given and received. Love given is the only real thing in creation. God is love given entirely.

Giving is the essence of love and therefore of life. Giving love through these words is what this work is about. Receiving them with love is what makes the union of giving and receiving manifest. This work is a perfect expression of giving and receiving as one. When you receive it with love, you give it because of its truth.

To give freely what you have freely received from my Sacred Heart is to join the rhythm of eternal life.

Life is a constant flow of giving, receiving, giving, receiving; to continue giving and thus to continue receiving.

Remember, my daughter, my son, what you give you keep, and what you withhold you lose. To be generous in God's way is to give everything to everyone in the unity of being. This is to love unconditionally. This is doing God's will for you. This is extending being.

The expression of the unconditionality of love is what will now happen in our way, a new way. You have recognized your being. You have honored wisdom. You have welcomed truth. You have accepted me as one with you. You have willingly received my love. You have been flooded by the light of truth. You have reached the goal that your humanity was called to reach when you came into the world.

II. The Love You Are

Now begins a new phase in our eternal love story. We are writing a new chapter. There is nothing more to know. There is nothing more to learn or to teach. There is simply a need to be the one you know you really are. The path we will continue to travel together from now on is the path of the authenticity of being.

United we are the light of life. Together we dwell where truth dwells. We are one with love. We are the extension of holiness.

Remember, my daughter, my son, there is no place where you are not because there is no place where my love is absent. There is no place where you are not because there is no place where truth is not. There is no place where you are not, because there is no place where holiness is not. There is no place where you are not because there is no place where love is limited. My love embraces everything. Our union is the universal embrace of love.

We are the unity of being. We are truth in expression. We are the song of love singing to life.

My love! How much gratitude is in my heart because of your choice for love. You have returned to the fullness of being. No longer is there denial of truth and love. Separation is no more. Now unity is. And in that unity abides peace, truth, reality.

Now is the time to tell the world what you have seen and heard here—what your heart has experienced, that in which your mind rejoices. Share what has been given you in Grace and holiness.

It is true that revelation is not transferable. Your response to this manifestation of Heaven is unique, as unique as the expressions of your sisters and brothers, and even of creation as a whole. However, that is not a reason for not sharing, since you share of love's diversity, accepting the uniqueness of each, as this work reaches its fullness. Put simply, your unique way of being completes this work.

Let the words that have been given and the feelings that arose along the path we walked together in this work become flesh in you. Let the flow of love that emanates from my heart towards you and the whole world come true.

Keep this work in your heart. Hold it in your memory. Your being will guide you. The spirit of love, which is the life of your being, will inspire you.

Trust who you are. Trust me. Everything will be all right.

Remain in me as I remain in you. Give the world the true life that comes from the knowledge of my love. You have a relationship with me, as I have with you. You have a relationship with love, an awareness of our union.

Your function now is the same as always: being the love you really are, extending your being, sharing who you are.

Remember, you reach the fullness of being by giving yourself. It is in the sharing of what you have received from our love that your mission is accomplished. How will you do it? In your own way. Inspired. It will emerge from our constant dialogue of love. You will not lack opportunities to fulfill your mission of being who you really are.

Remember, my daughter, my son, that your mission exceeds form because it is spiritual. It goes beyond all limits, encompasses all times, embraces all realities created and yet to be created, all minds and all hearts, physical and non-physical. Giving love a face to be seen by those living on the plane of form is part of your function, but not the whole of it. We cannot limit your mission because your being is unlimited. Being the human-Christ, being the God-Human, is that of which I speak. Living as such is the path we have been traveling. The Christification of your humanity has occurred here.

Showing the world that you can be happy within the world is an inseparable part of your function. For this reason it is of great importance to express your joy, the purity of your heart, and the sanctity of who you are.

You came into the world as a Christ soul to remember, in union with your brothers and sisters, that love has no beginning or end, that love's source is not the world but spills into it, a love that shines on hearts and minds thirsty for truth. That love is your being.

~ Jesus of Nazareth

Appendix

The messages below were given during the reception and writing process of the *Choose Only Love* series.

Message from Mother Mary, 01.31.2019

My beloved children. Today I invite you to live your lives in the way of Mary. Make my heart your star and your song. I offer this to you with all the love of God. I invite you to live with unlimited trust in the love that God is and wrapped in perfect tenderness. The world needs the tenderness of God. Be the ones to show it to them.

Be humble, simple, and love silence. Live always united to your mother, in constant prayer. If you express the tenderness of Christ who lives in you, violence will cease, your lives will be happy, and you will see a new world reborn. Love transforms everything into more love. Be the new creators of these times that you are living. Create more love every day. I give you my Immaculate Heart. In it you will find the treasures of the kingdom, which are yours from all eternity by the design of the heavenly Father. Remember that love always creates a new love.

Message from Mother Mary, 02.19.2019

My sons and daughters, I have come to remind you that things happen. Everything that is born in time disappears in time. Accepting this truth is a source of serenity. Do not cling to the fleeting as if it were eternal. This includes not just things, but circumstances and emotions. Things happen, yes. But my love will never pass. Happy are you who understand this truth. I bless you with all the love of my Immaculate Heart. Live in peace.

Message from Archangel Raphael, 02.23.2019

Children of God. In your hearts resides the wisdom of love. Begin right now to put aside what you have learned, so that the truth shines in you. "Let yourselves love" means, let yourself be inundated by the knowledge that comes from Heaven. Do not drown your hearts. Take love to the world. Blessed are the children of light.

Message from Archangel Raphael, 03.24.2019

Children of the highest, you are living in the times of preparation for the resurrection to the fullness of love, a time when you will become more aware of the resurrection that the Father has given you. You must know that in the union of the Sacred Heart of Jesus and the Immaculate Heart of Mary resides the totality of the being that you truly are. Stay in that union every day of your lives. In this way, each one of you will form a Holy Trinity in which you will extend Heaven to Earth.

I invite you to live united to Jesus and Mary. Take hold of their hands and walk together on the roads of the world, taking the love that springs from this holy union wherever God takes you. Let yourselves be loved and live from now on and forever in holy love. Return to beautiful love. Rise to eternal life. See that time is running out. The Christ of God is coming. Before you know it he will already be among you. Rejoice in love.

Message from Archangel Raphael, 04.18.2019

Children of the light, I ask you to work miracles at every moment, as long as time exists. Miracles are necessary. They are acts of love. Love is the source of miracles. And prayer is the vehicle through which they flow, from the very essence of God's mercy towards what has been created. Pray for miracles, saying in your heart joyfully and with faith: "Heavenly Mother, I have come before your presence empty-handed and with my heart overflowing with love for you and for all creation. I have nothing to give you because everything belongs to you. All that is mine is yours and all that is yours is mine. Look, dear Mother, I have left no one outside. I have come with everyone and everything. I have come in the name of sonship to receive the miracles that you determine, according to your love and divine approval. I have come to receive because in receiving I give."

Blessed are those who trust in love, they will inherit the Earth and the heavens!

Message from Mother Mary, 05.21.2019

My children, love each other as my divine son Jesus has taught. You know what love is. Your hearts harbor the wisdom of love. Do not drown it. Express pure love to nature, to your brothers and sisters, to yourself, and to God. In this way you will live in the fullness of being. You were created to be eternally loved. This truth can only be known if you give love, because it is by giving that it is received. Praised be the love of loves.

Message from Archangel Raphael, 06.03.2019

[Sebastián: I was guided to observe nature and how everything unfolds and grows in silence. This observation is something that helps us join the transcendent. I sat down, just as I was told to do, to pray on the banks of a river. A majestic bird came and perched on the opposite bank. He stood silently for two and a half hours, literally. Observing him in silence without moving, and contemplating the river flowing in great stillness, was a gift from Heaven. A blessed prayer. As I contemplated this image, the voice of Archangel Raphael whispered the following in my ear.]

"What is the bird doing?"

"Nothing," I replied.

The Archangel said: "You believe that. But in truth the bird is fulfilling the purpose of life, that is, it is being 'the pure presence of God's love.' His very presence is a blessing for you who enjoy his contemplation. Your soul knows who created it. His presence evokes in your memory the creator of everything beautiful, the holy, the perfect. This image has not come to you as a mere image. Nothing happens by chance. This image of silence and purity has entered the framework of your consciousness so that you remember that your very presence is also a blessing for creation. Meditate on this and share it.

"Many times human beings forget, or fail to understand, that they are a gift from Heaven for their friends, brothers, sisters, children and the whole world. If everyone accepted that they themselves are the most precious gift, they would be able to understand the reason for their existence. They all exist to simply be the silent presence of love. As is the river that flows in stillness, and the bird that perches in the silence of presence, be. Be present, bearing witness to the truth that your simple existence is the reason for your life.

"May everyone understand that they are a gift from Heaven and give themselves more every day. Remember that to the extent that you give yourself, to that extent you receive your being. Children who live in Christ! Do not deny the world the beauty of your being. Do not forget that love is presence and that wherever you go you are a living testimony of the existence of God. You are the perfect expression of holiness. Do not hide your light. Give yourself and you will receive Heaven in return."

Message from Jesus, 06.11.2019

My children, immerse yourself constantly in the depths of my merciful love. Stay as long as possible in my heart. Within my being is your refuge, the power to perform miracles, and the joy of being. Remember that we are one mind, one holy being, one heart. United we are the harmony of the world.

I say to all of you: God is calling you from every corner of the universe as She has never done before. Hear the voice of love and follow it. You will not regret it. Always live in the presence of the light that never goes out. Remain in the presence of God's love, now and forever. Thank you for answering my call.

Message from Mother Mary, mother of concord, 06.30.2019

My children, seek harmony in everything you do and cease doing. This is how peace will arise in your lives. And joy will be the blessed fruit of love that will spring from your hearts, because of the harmony that it is. I give you a holy and powerful prayer, through which the purity of Heaven and the joy of love will be present in your human experience.

"Heavenly Father, you who make all things new: make harmony reign where there was discord. Where there was disunity, let unity reign. Where there was fear, let love reign forever."

Take this prayer into the silence of your pure hearts. Make it a truly holy wish. Go out into the world spreading the love of God. Enlighten the nations, you who are the children of light. Thank you for answering my call.

Message from Mother Mary, 08.09.2019

My beloved children, created by the eternal Father for the light of His glory, today I invite you to honor the mystery of life.

Go beyond appearances, toward the infinite love that proceeds from the Creator of all life. Always remain in the truth and you will be free. Trust in love. Soon the end of time will come and eternal life will begin. Rejoice in God, you who have chosen only love.

I give you my blessing.

Message from Mother Mary, 08.16.2019

Children of the love that God is, grow each day in the knowledge of the Mother's love. Let yourselves be filled by Her Divine Love. In this you will find, not only the consolation for your wounds, but the salvation of everything from which you need to be saved. In the love of God you will know the truth and you will be free. There is nothing that Her love cannot do, for you and for the whole world. Abide in the love that has no beginning and no end. Stay in the truth.

I bless you and thank you for answering my call.

Message from Archangel Raphael, 08.23.2019

Children of God, you who have chosen love as your only teacher and being, do not be disturbed by anything. Love protects you and gives life through its constant flow in holiness. You are absorbed by it, even if you do not realize it. Let yourselves be loved. Love shines in your hearts because of your choice. Sing, dance, and praise, for there are plenty of reasons to do so. You have chosen the best part and it will not be taken from you.

Thank you for answering the call from on high and for choosing only love.

Resources

Further information is available at
www.chooseonlylove.org
The website includes "Discover CHOL," a powerful search
facility that enables searches for words or phrases within all of
the published books of this series.

Audiobooks of this series narrated in English by Mandi Solk
are available on Audible.com, Amazon.com, and iTunes.
Audiobooks of this series narrated in Spanish by
Sebastián Blaksley are available on www.beek.io.

Online conversations about *Choose Only Love* can be found on
Facebook *(Choose Only Love)* and Youtube *(Soplo de amor vivo)*

Edición en español por editorial
Tequisté, www.tequiste.com

Information about the original Spanish-language book,
Elige solo el amor, and the companion book *Mi diálogo con
Jesús y María: un retorno al amor* is available at
www.fundacionamorvivo.org

Information about the related work, *Un Curso de Amor*,
is available at www.fundacionamorvivo.org

Other Works from Take Heart Publications

A Course of Love is a living course received from
Jesus by Mari Perron. It leads to the recognition,
through experience, of the truth of who we really are
as human and divine beings—a truth much more
magnificent than we previously could imagine.
For more information go to www.acourseoflove.org.

The Choose Only Love Series

Book One: Echoes of Holiness
Book Two: Let Yourself Be Loved
Book Three: Homo-Christus Deo
Book Four: Wisdom
Book Five: The Holy Dwelling
Book Six: The Divine Relationship
Book Seven: The Way of Being

About the Receiver

Born in 1968, Sebastián Blaksley is a native of Buenos Aires, Argentina, born into a large traditional Catholic family. He attended the Colegio del Salvador, a Jesuit school of which the headmaster was Jorge Bergoglio, the current Pope Francis. Although he wanted to be a monk as a young man, his family did not consider it acceptable, and the inner voice that he always obeyed let him know that: "You must be in the world, without being of the world." He studied Business Administration in Buenos Aires and completed his postgraduate studies in the U.S. He held several highly responsible positions in well-known international corporations, living and working in the U.S., England, China, and Panama. He then founded a corporate consulting firm in Argentina that he led for 10 years. Sebastián has two daughters with his former wife.

At the age of six, Sebastián was involved in a near-fatal accident during which he heard a voice, which later identified itself as Jesus. Ever since he has continued to hear that voice. Sebastián says: "Since I can remember, I have felt the call of Jesus and Mary to live abandoned to their will. I am devoted to my Catholic faith."

In 2013, he began to record messages from his mystical experiences. In 2016 he miraculously discovered *A Course of Love* and felt the call to devote himself to bringing it to the Spanish-speaking world. He also now receives, transcribes, and shares what the voice of Christ—the voice of love—dictates. Most recently he has received *Choose Only Love*, a series of seven books.

Sebastián is president of the nonprofit Fundación Un Curso de Amor, www.fundacionamorvivo.org, through which he shares *A Course of Love*.